IBD'S 10 SECRETS TO SUCCESS

Investor's Business Daily has spent years analyzing leaders and successful people in all walks of life. Most have 10 traits that, when combined, can turn dreams into reality. Each day, we highlight one.

1 **HOW YOU THINK IS EVERYTHING:** Always be positive. Think success, not failure. Beware of a negative environment.

2 **DECIDE UPON YOUR TRUE DREAMS AND GOALS:** Write down your specific goals and develop a plan to reach them.

3 **TAKE ACTION:** Goals are nothing without action. Don't be afraid to get started. Just do it.

4 **NEVER STOP LEARNING:** Go back to school or read books. Get training and acquire skills.

5 **BE PERSISTENT AND WORK HARD:** Success is a marathon, not a sprint. Never give up.

6 **LEARN TO ANALYZE DETAILS:** Get all the facts, all the input. Learn from your mistakes.

7 **FOCUS YOUR TIME AND MONEY:** Don't let other people or things distract you.

8 **DON'T BE AFRAID TO INNOVATE; BE DIFFERENT:** Following the herd is a sure way to mediocrity.

9 **DEAL AND COMMUNICATE WITH PEOPLE EFFECTIVELY:** No person is an island. Learn to understand and motivate others.

10 **BE HONEST AND DEPENDABLE; TAKE RESPONSIBILITY:** Otherwise, Nos. 1-9 won't matter.

What *Investor's Business Daily* Readers Have to Say About the "Leaders & Success" Section

I am a mentor to a young boy, 13, who has no Dad. I have met with him weekly for three years. I use the "Leaders & Success" section to develop messages for him that he can apply to his benefit. That this is working is no surprise I am sure, for as we think so we are. But now that several of his friends have joined in these discussions, it has been doubly gratifying.

— Michael Burton

"Leaders & Success" is an important part of my mornings. It is an inspirational tool that I utilize not only to assure that I begin my days on a positive note, but it gives me food for thought.

— Jim Elder

My daughter in the 5th grade reads a "Leaders & Success" bio from *Investor's Business Daily* every day as I drive her to school. What an education she is getting.

— Michael McLennan

"Leaders & Success" is read by my 15-year-old and his friends daily. Keep up the good work.

— Peter Siracusa

I love the "Leaders & Success" section as it gives inspiration to me to go ahead in my life and to think about life in a positive and successful way.

— Veera Reddy

Military and Political Leaders & Success

Other McGraw-Hill Books by William J. O'Neil

The Successful Investor: What 80 Million People Need to Know to Invest Profitably and Avoid Big Losses

Business Leaders & Success: 55 Top Business Leaders & How They Achieved Greatness

Sports Leaders & Success: 55 Top Sports Leaders & How They Achieved Greatness

How to Make Money in Stocks: A Winning System in Good Times or Bad

24 Essential Lessons for Investment Success: Learn the Most Important Investment Techniques from the Founder of Investor's Business Daily

Military and Political Leaders & Success

55 Top Military and Political Leaders & How They Achieved Greatness

Introduction by William J. O'Neil

McGraw-Hill

New York   Chicago   San Francisco   Lisbon   London
Madrid   Mexico City   Milan   New Delhi   San Juan
Seoul   Singapore   Sydney   Toronto

Copyright © 2005 by William J. O'Neil. All rights reserved. Printed in the United States of America. Except as permitted under the United States Copyright Act of 1976, no part of this publication may be reproduced or distributed in any form or by any means, or stored in a database or retrieval system, without the prior written permission of the publisher.

2 3 4 5 6 7 8 9 0   DOC/DOC   0 9 8 7 6 5 4

ISBN 0-07-144059-3

McGraw-Hill books are available at special quantity discounts to use as premiums and sales promotions, or for use in corporate training programs. For more information, please write to the Director of Special Sales, Professional Publishing, McGraw-Hill, Two Penn Plaza, New York, NY 10121-2298. Or contact your local bookstore.

This book is printed on recycled, acid-free paper containing a minimum of 50% recycled, de-inked fiber.

Library of Congress Cataloging-in-Publication Data
Military and political leaders & success : 55 top military and political leaders & how they achieved greatness / with an introduction by William J. O'Neil.—1st ed.
     p.   cm.
Includes index.
   ISBN 0-07-144059-3 (alk. paper)
   1. Military biography.   2. Statesmen—Biography.   3. Leadership.   4. Success.
   5. Nobility of character.   I. Investor's business daily.
U51.M54 2004
658.4'092—dc22

                                                                2004005287

Contents

Introduction

Successful people in all fields share similar qualities that move them to the top — determination, hard work and learning from their failures, for instance. Yet each has a different approach and consequently a unique edge.

Investor's Business Daily's "Leaders & Success" section illustrates exactly how these people became successful, so you can apply their tips, traits and experiences to your life. Every one of these leaders has a story with lessons we can learn.

In this collection of *Military and Political Leaders & Success*, learn how Colin Powell achieved the highest military post in the land with a determined will to excel as a soldier, backed up by the necessary courage, integrity, and hard work to make it happen. Discover how Prussian officer Karl von Clausewitz wrote the definitive military text for modern warfare, influencing such military lights as Dwight D. Eisenhower, George Patton and Colin Powell. Find out how Poland's Lech Walesa united and led a 10-million-strong labor union to democracy, rising above imprisonment and government bans. And rediscover how George Washington used his British military experience to free the American colonies, then applied wisdom and restraint as the first United States president, forever earning his place as the Father of the Nation.

You'll also learn how successful leaders set and pursue goals. Sometimes they are big, sometimes small, but when these determined individuals decide something needs to be done, they find a way to do it.

Often times, their greatest accomplishments are a response to the world around them — a war needs to be won, a wrong needs to be righted, a political system needs to be changed — but they wouldn't be able to influence history-making events if they hadn't, all along, been giving 100 percent to the smaller goals that eventually add up to greatness.

Winston Churchill found his greatest success in saving the free world from Nazi domination, but not before he had served in the army, in Parliament, and in several key government positions, including head of Britain's navy. He'd spent much of his adult life reading and writing about history and military exploits, knowledge that served him well in his stand against Germany. He spent the years before World War II largely as a political outcast, insisting that a man named Hitler was an evil tyrant when a war-weary world wanted to believe Hitler when he said he was not. When the world finally woke up and all of Western Europe except England had fallen, they turned to the man who had tried to warn them. Churchill was ready.

Abraham Lincoln's political career often reads like a blueprint for failure. He lost more often than he won in three decades of running for office, but he didn't let that keep him down. When the Missouri Compromise (outlawing slavery in certain new states) was repealed in 1854, Lincoln got back into the race to do something about it. He subsequently lost in two attempts for the U.S. Senate and in one for the Republican vice presidential candidacy, but Lincoln succeeded in getting his message out, most famously in his "House Divided" speech: "I believe this government cannot endure permanently half slave and half free. I do not expect the Union to be dissolved — I do not expect the house to fall — but I do expect it will cease to be divided."

The time had come for such a message, and Lincoln was narrowly elected president in 1860. Entering the White House under threat of assassination — a permanent condition of his presidency that ultimately came to pass — Lincoln kept the Union together despite constant blunders by high-ranking military officers, Cabinet members who regarded him as a backwater simpleton, and foreign interference and intrigue. In the process, he succeeded in abolishing slavery, the greatest contradiction to our American creed of freedom and justice for all. Abraham Lincoln thus earned his place in history as "The Great Emancipator."

George S. Patton was a career soldier who had built his reputation long before World War II called him to his greatest test and glory. A young enthusiast of military history, Patton overcame dyslexia to graduate from the U.S. Military Academy. An expert cavalryman who literally wrote the book on saber fighting, Patton immediately recognized emerging tank technology as the vehicle of future warfare. So when he was assigned to tank school during World War I, Patton turned in his saddle and led his tank brigade in key battles at the war's end. Patton's ability to adjust to changing circumstances, his attitude that he would win because he would not fail, defined his career and contributed greatly to Allied victory in the Second World War.

No task was beneath Patton. He regarded his soldiers as the most important element of warfare. He didn't care who got the credit, so long as the job was done. In North Africa and Sicily, the job was done, as Patton's soldiers fought their way to victory. His Third Army fought on against the massive German effort to push back the Allies, known as the "Battle of the Bulge." While others panicked as the Nazis advanced 50 miles into Allied territory, Patton saw opportunity. He had enough confidence in his well-trained men and in his tank expertise to outflank the Germans in two days, effectively ending their last stand against the Allies. Having fulfilled his childhood ambition to become a hero, Patton stands as one of history's greatest military commanders.

Nelson Mandela's entire life was dedicated to ridding South Africa of apartheid, the racially divisive system that treated black South Africans as second-class citizens. At age 76, Mandela became that country's first black democratically elected president after more than half a century of working, agitating, writing and speaking for justice. He started out as a lawyer and ended up in prison for 27 years, refusing offers of release on the condition that he renounce his position. His selfless integrity made Mandela a symbolic lightning rod around which the anti-apartheid movement ultimately prevailed.

Ronald Reagan went into politics after a career as an actor because he wanted to change the world for the better. A major part of this plan was to end the Cold War. Reagan had studied Soviet-American relations for decades, and he thought that détente, whereby the U.S. and the U.S.S.R. built up weapons that they so far hadn't used on each other because mutual destruction would surely follow, was a sorry excuse for foreign policy. So, when he became U.S. president, Reagan called the Soviet Union's bluff and challenged their already-tottering economy to a renewed arms race of defensive weapons. He also challenged Premier Gorbachev to tear down the Berlin Wall, the "iron curtain" that had literally separated the communist from the free world. One year after Reagan left office, that wall came down. Two years later, the Soviet Union did, too.

None of these great leaders started out knowing they would one day change the world, but all of them learned from their history books how such change is possible. On the campaign trail, Harry Truman once said, "Not all readers become leaders, but all leaders must be readers." That is exactly what all of these great leaders were, and as you read on, you'll discover why people who hope to successfully influence what goes on around them will develop the habit of reading great books.

"Leaders & Success" focuses specifically on biography for a very good reason. We have learned that from Alexander the Great to Napoleon to George Patton, the examples of the most successful leaders in history have had a profound effect on the history yet to come. Patton liked to quote Napoleon, who said, "The only right way of learning the science of war is to read and reread the campaigns of the great captains." There is no secret to success. Future leaders study past leaders to understand the timeless qualities behind rising to — and wisely administering — power. We hope their examples inspire you, too, as you learn what it takes to succeed from some of the greatest political and military leaders of all time.

Acknowledgments

There are no secrets to success. It is the result of preparation, hard work, and learning from failure.

— GEN. COLIN POWELL

No book makes its way into the reader's hands without the strong commitment of a dedicated and talented team. Many thanks are extended to those individuals who contributed their time and talents to the completion of this book. Specifically, Joannè von Alroth, Sally Doyle, Sue Frazer, Cynthia Martin, Chris Gessel, Susan Warfel, and the copy editors of *Investor's Business Daily,* and Donya Dickerson and Jane Palmieri of McGraw-Hill, for their careful guidance and support to this encouraging book. And I would especially like to thank Sharon Brooks and Shana Smith for their exemplary editorial guidance.

William J. O'Neil
Founder of *Investor's Business Daily*

PART 1

Winning Through Discipline And Determination

©CORBIS

Nothing in the world could take the place of persistence. Talent will not; nothing is more common than unsuccessful men with talent. Genius will not; unrewarded genius is almost a proverb. Education will not; the world is full of educated derelicts. Persistence and determination are omnipotent.

— CALVIN COOLIDGE

1

President Dwight D. Eisenhower
Hard Work And Delegation Helped Him Steer Our Nation

It was a simple envelope that tipped off Dwight D. Eisenhower that the White House he'd just inherited was in desperate need of a top-to-bottom reorganization.

The 34th president was only a few hours into his new job in 1953 when the chief usher handed him a sealed envelope. To the five-star general and victorious commander of the Allied forces in World War II, this act spoke volumes about inefficiency and lack of organization. Hundreds of letters arrived at the White House each day. Was this the best use of time for the leader of the Free World?

"Never bring me a sealed envelope," Eisenhower (1890–1965) told the White House staffer. "That's what I've got aides for."

Pop wisdom today tells us not to sweat the small things. Not so with Eisenhower. "Ike," as he was called, knew that small things told big stories. As an Army officer, Eisenhower would inspect a single company of men to learn the status of the entire regiment. His read on the envelope incident helped launch a systems makeover.

This incident, as recounted in Geoffrey Perret's 1999 biography "Eisenhower," shows the high priority Ike placed on organization. From it, he knew, came good performance. It was a crucial element in the role he played in American history — as president from 1953 to 1961 and as victorious Allied military commander in World War II.

It's what let him carry out the events of June 6, 1944 — coordinating 5,000 ships, 11,000 planes and 150,000 men sent to battle on D-Day to liberate Europe from the Nazis.

"He was very organized and streamlined a lot of what he did to make things more efficient," said David Coleman, assistant professor at the Miller Center for Public Affairs at the University of Virginia. That, according to Coleman, gave Eisenhower a sense of confidence, in both his plan and in his staff. He knew his staff would carry out his decisions.

Streamlining The System

A man of integrity, hard work and duty to country, Eisenhower — when handed a task — began at the beginning.

In 1953, he started with the White House. He told his staff he wanted to spend his time only on those problems that others couldn't solve. He created two staffs, one personal and the other presidential, so that all his needs were taken care of. This system became the standard practice.

Memos were to be kept to a single page, he said, and any letter received from a member of Congress was to be summarized into a single line. From this summary, Ike decided if he needed to spend more time reading the entire letter. He signed the thousands of documents requiring his signature using only his initials DE in order to save more time, according to Perret. To stay atop the vast workings of the federal government, Ike asked for a daily summary of the 40 most important government actions taken the previous day.

"Leadership," said Eisenhower, was "the art of getting someone else to do something you want done because he wants to do it."

As a military commander, Ike depended on his staff to bring him vital input and create options from which he could choose the best. This created a competitive spirit among his team, making members want to excel.

He used the same system as president. With the Cold War taking shape, Ike needed a Soviet policy. So he created three competing task forces to form alternative strategies. On a single day, all three met in the White House library and briefed Ike on their findings. Ike selected elements from all three task forces and from that fashioned America's foreign policy toward the Soviets.

Accepting criticism was an important part in Ike's planning. In a pre-D-Day briefing for the British, attended by British Prime Minister Winston Churchill, King George VI and 150 British force commanders, Ike first briefed the group on the cross-channel operation, then asked his audience to speak up with criticism.

"I consider it to be the duty of anyone who sees a flaw in the plan not to hesitate to say so," Eisenhower announced to the British military leaders sitting in the university lecture hall turned battle-planning room. "I have no sympathy with anyone, whatever his station, who will not brook criticism. We are here to get the best possible results."

Ike always asked for a variety of input to help him think through complex issues. He let his people know that their input was to be free of self-interest. At his Friday White House Cabinet meetings, Ike asked the secretaries to present him with options that were best for the country. He didn't want to know about their own department's needs. They were to be statesmen, he told them, not salesmen.

Reverse Psychology

Ike's personal style, learned from working with Gen. Douglas MacArthur, was to keep his options open by criticizing the ideas he agreed with and showing enthusiasm for the ideas he didn't. Such tactics brought out the best ideas through rigorous debate but without making him show his hand too early.

To Eisenhower, continuing education was key. Overseeing the complex U.S. economy, Ike took to studying newspaper financial pages. He also sought advice from friends and successful investors such as Bernard Baruch, who made a fortune in the stock market before 30. Ike's philosophy was the more free enterprise the better and as little government as possible.

Hard work was another touchstone. As commander of the European theater of operations, Ike shunned the more relaxed work attitude held by some of the European commanders and was at his desk early. He often ate lunch there and came in on Sundays for a few hours.

His mother told him as a boy, "He that conquers his own soul is greater than he that conquers a city." At that time, his soul conquering began at 4:30 a.m., when he had to get out of bed to start the kitchen-stove fire on the family farm.

By the time he was president, Ike's schedule started when he got up at 6 a.m., read the intelligence folder and skimmed three papers — the *New York Times, New York Herald* and *Washington Post*. He had breakfast by 7:15 a.m. and was at his desk by 8 a.m. He broke for lunch, then was back to work until 3:30 p.m., when he played a little golf. He was back at his desk until 6 p.m., where he left it spanking clean for the next morning.

Facing and learning from criticism was an art that Ike learned over time. He would face down some of the toughest opponents, including Churchill.

But he allowed his opponents to have their say. With Churchill, that once involved a six-hour appeal that a World War II invasion operation, called "Anvil," shouldn't take place. Churchill threatened to resign. But Ike said it had to take place, and that was that. Perret makes the point that Eisenhower "stood up once again to poetry, personality and prime ministerial tears."

Eisenhower was a determined leader. A smoker, averaging four packs of cigarettes a day, Ike quit cold turkey one day, "by simply giving himself an order." Such discipline came from the small-town values learned growing up on the family farm in Abilene, Kan., where he picked vegetables, collected eggs, fed horses and milked cows.

He also believed life should include joy. "Unless each day can be looked back upon as one in which you have had some fun, some joy, some satisfaction — that day is a loss," he told students at Dartmouth College.

2

Founding Father Thomas Jefferson

His Reputation Was Built On Hard Work, Education And Humility

At 33, Thomas Jefferson was already well suited for his task of writing the Declaration of Independence, a job given to him by his fellow members of the Second Continental Congress in 1776.

Highly educated and intellectually curious, Jefferson studied the words of history's greatest thinkers, including Francis Bacon, Sir Isaac Newton and John Locke. These men were three of the philosophers of Europe's intellectual revolution known as the "Enlightenment." The foundation of the Enlightenment was that educated people were capable of governing themselves and therefore didn't need rulers.

In roughly two weeks, Jefferson wrote the declaration. "It would eventually become the most cherished document in American history," wrote Noble Cunningham in "In Pursuit of Reason: The Life of Thomas Jefferson." The Continental Congress adopted the declaration on July 4, 1776.

When some fellow signatories of the declaration speculated that Jefferson had borrowed from other authors' works and thoughts in writing it, Jefferson denied the charge, while acknowledging his lifetime of accumulated knowledge.

"I did not consider it as any part of my charge to invent new ideas altogether, and to offer no sentiment which had ever been expressed before," Jefferson said.

The American Mind

Jefferson (1743–1826) said his objective was "to place before mankind the common sense of the subject, in terms so plain and firm as to command their assent (for independence)." He further said that the declaration was "neither aiming at originality of principle or sentiment, nor yet copied from any particular and previous writing, it was intended to be an expression of the American mind."

In the declaration, Jefferson first laid out the reasoning of the American colonies' action of declaring their independence from England. He asserted "that all men are created equal" and all have certain "inalienable rights" bestowed on them. These rights, which he listed as "life, liberty, and the pursuit of happiness," were entrusted by citizens to governments for protection. "Whenever any form of government becomes destructive of these ends, it is the right of the people to alter or to abolish it, and to institute new government."

He then outlined specific grievances against King George III of England. Jefferson concluded the declaration with a stirring resolve of his fellow signatories' commitment to their cause: "And for the support of this declaration, with a firm reliance on the protection of Divine Providence, we mutually pledge to each other our lives, our fortunes, and our sacred honor."

The legacy of the Declaration of Independence is significant. It lent support to the ideals of the French Revolution. It inspired, among other great leaders, Indian organizer Mohandas Gandhi.

For fear of alienating Southern slave-holding states, the Continental Congress deleted from the declaration an original passage of Jefferson's that strongly condemned slavery. During his career, Jefferson wrote often and strongly of slavery's evil and advocated its end, despite the contradiction of owning slaves himself.

"One should not blame Jefferson for falling short of perfection as a liberator of the human spirit," Fawn Brodie, a modern biographer of Jefferson, said in "Thomas Jefferson: Architect of Democracy," by John Severance. "He continued to follow traditions that were in his time practically universal." After his death, his intellectual legacy served to aid the liberation of both women and blacks.

"Jefferson's thoughtful demeanor was impressive," said longtime rival and friend John Adams, who first got to know Jefferson in the Second Continental Congress. "(Jefferson) was so prompt, frank, explicit and decisive upon committees and in conversation that he soon seized upon my heart," Adams said.

Jefferson was the son of a successful planter and surveyor who went on to be elected to Virginia's House of Burgess. Thomas was only 14 when his father died and left him the wealth of 2,500 acres of land. He learned a lesson from his father that would last his lifetime and contribute to his legacy as one of the world's greatest thinkers.

"My father's education had been quite neglected; but being of a strong mind, sound judgment and eager after information, he read much and improved himself," Jefferson said.

His lifetime commitment to education culminated in his founding of the University of Virginia in 1825. It was one of three things Jefferson wanted as an epitaph on his gravestone (the other two being his authorship of the Declaration of Independence and of the Statute of Virginia for Religious Freedom).

"Education for everyone," Jefferson said, "is the true corrective of abuses of constitutional power."

Jefferson managed his time with care since he was a young man. He typically rose at 5 a.m. most of his adult life and retired around 10 p.m.

"Determine never to be idle. No person will have occasion to complain of the want of time, who never loses any. It is wonderful how much may be done, if we are always doing," Jefferson advised in a letter to his daughter.

No Nonsense

Jefferson, our third president, believed that as a legislator, he was a servant of the people, and he conducted himself accordingly. At his inauguration he shunned the fancy clothes and sword that his predecessors, George Washington and John Adams, had worn to theirs. Jefferson's garb, noted a reporter at the time, was, as usual, that of a plain citizen without any distinctive badge of office.

"When brought together in society, all are perfectly equal, whether foreign or domestic, titled or untitled, in or out of office," Jefferson told his administration.

While Jefferson believed in the democratic spoils of majority rule, he thought a just government didn't forget the minority has rights that must also be safeguarded.

From the outset of his presidency, Jefferson made it clear he'd be in charge of his administration and that he'd take responsibility for its actions, Cunningham wrote.

"My confidence in my countrymen generally leaves me without much fear for the future," Jefferson said.

He died on July 4, 1826, the 50th anniversary of the Declaration of Independence.

3

Rome's Julius Caesar

Total Focus On His Goal

Made Him Emperor

How did Julius Caesar become one of the greatest leaders of the ancient world? He never worried about decisions after making them.

When Caesar held junior political power in Rome in 65 B.C., he organized gladiatorial games featuring slaves who were seen as a threat to Rome.

He also had memorials of war victories by his uncle, Marius, re-erected in the Forum. Rome's top political officials still supported L. Cornelius Sulla, a one-time rival of Marius.

An irate Senate condemned Caesar's actions. He won popularity, though, from Rome's common people. They were pleased with both of his decisions.

His military maneuvers were daring. Stationed in Gaul just north of Italy in 49 B.C., he marched his army to the Rubicon River, which divided the territories. He was short on troops, and his enemies thought he would wait for more legions to arrive before moving southward and trying to overthrow the Roman Republic.

But Caesar crossed the Rubicon and raced to Rome. He proceeded to crush Pompey in a civil war.

"Possessed of a magnetic personality and boundless egotism, he lacked both fear and scruple; a man whose end governed his means, and a man who would allow nothing to stand in his way," J.F.C. Fuller wrote in "Julius Caesar: Man, Soldier and Tyrant."

Reformer, Ruler

Caesar (100–44 B.C.) introduced governmental reforms that were the basis of Rome's administration for centuries. He served with Pompey and Crassus in the Triumvirate that ruled Rome from 60 to 49 B.C., and he was sole dictator from 49 B.C. until he was assassinated.

His military victories made Rome the top European power.

Unlike other Roman leaders, he showed a ruthless ambition to achieve his goals, no matter the cost. He sometimes used unscrupulous means to get what he wanted. He pushed successfully for political reforms while sometimes undermining fellow politicians. He had one goal in mind: power.

Caesar became popular in Rome soon after entering politics around 75 B.C. He did so by maintaining public buildings and organizing festivals.

He borrowed money from Crassus, the wealthiest man in Rome, and spent it to provide entertainment for Roman citizens. He showed a special talent for putting his opponents in the wrong and making them appear as absurd fanatics, wrote Matthias Gelzer in "Caesar: Politician and Statesman."

"Caesar also possessed statesmanlike qualities. He had a quick grasp of and prompt reaction to the circumstances with which he (was) faced," Gelzer wrote, "and a creative political ability, which can lead the statesman's contemporaries in new directions and itself create new circumstances."

He was a military genius. During the Gallic wars (58 to 50 B.C.), which extended Rome's empire to the Atlantic Ocean, he won nine battles and lost only two in which he personally took part. His defeat of Pompey ended the Roman Republic and paved the way for later Roman emperors.

Two of his keys to victory were surprise and rapid movement.

After Pompey fled Italy in the civil war, Caesar chased him to Spain and defeated him in just 40 days. Caesar then raced to Brundisium on Italy's southeast coast.

Despite cold weather, insufficient supplies and the lack of several of his legions, he told his men, "I consider rapidity of movement the best substitute for all of these things. The most potent thing in war is the unexpected." He crossed the Adriatic Sea into Greece and destroyed the rest of Pompey's forces.

The Roman biographer Suetonius once wrote: "(Caesar) joined the battle, not only after planning his movements in advance but on a sudden opportunity . . . when one would least expect him to make a move."

Gaius Julius Caesar was born in Rome to an aristocratic family. His education centered on public life and oratory. His tutor was Marcus Antonius Gnipho, a master of Greek and Latin rhetoric.

Caesar wrote verses and developed an effective style of public speaking. He used a "pure, plain language and a somewhat high-pitched delivery accompanied by vigorous gesticulation," Michael Grant wrote in "Julius Caesar."

Caesar practiced his oratorical skills as a prosecutor. In 77 B.C., a leading Sullan, Gnaeus Cornelius Dolabella, was brought up on charges of extortion. Two talented lawyers defended Dolabella, who was acquitted.

"Nevertheless, Caesar worked up his speeches into an imposing document, which survived as a literary masterpiece and won (Caesar) a reputation as one of Rome's leading orators," Gelzer wrote.

Caesar spouted self-confidence. He was sailing on the Mediterranean Sea in 74 B.C., when pirates captured his ship. They realized that he was a nobleman and tried to get a huge ransom of 20 talents. He was offended and offered 50 talents.

A Cheeky Captive

While waiting on an island for Roman officials to pay the ransom, Caesar was disrespectful toward his captors. He demanded undisturbed quiet while composing themes in verse and prose. He recited his work to the pirates, but when they were unappreciative of it, he called them barbarians. "He said the pirates were incompetent with weapons. Caesar induced among the pirates as much fear as respect," Roman historian Velleius Paterculus once wrote.

Roman officials paid the ransom. But Caesar promised that he'd return and execute the pirates, who laughed at the threat.

With no official authority, he led a group of warships that tracked down the pirates. They were captured and crucified in the hot Mediterranean sun. Before they were affixed to the crosses, however, their throats were slit to kill them.

"The unrelenting punishment and the avoidance of unnecessary suffering are equally typical of Caesar's ruthless realism," Alfred Duggan wrote in "Julius Caesar: A Great Life in Brief." "His justice was never merciful, but he never went out of his way to inflict pain for fun."

4

Prime Minister Margaret Thatcher

Her Principled Determination Turned Britain Around

Most people think of former British Prime Minister Margaret Thatcher as the "Iron Lady." That label was first stuck on her in the mid-1970s by the Soviet army journal *Red Star*. It lambasted her for a speech in which she said detente would lead to defeat of democracies of the West.

Thatcher didn't back down. "Her determination was one of the qualities most responsible for her successes," said Tim Knox, editor at the Centre for Policy Studies, a British think tank Thatcher helped set up.

Her resolution helped Thatcher to become the longest-serving premier in the 20th century. Her policies helped change the face of Britain — and the world.

Hard work was a constant for Thatcher. She came from a middle-class home and a small-business background. Her father, Alfred Roberts, bought a food shop and then opened several more in the town of Grantham. His wife and two daughters helped out when needed.

Roberts was Thatcher's first model in politics. He felt it was part of civic duty. He served for several years as the mayor of Grantham, where Thatcher was born in 1925.

Perhaps the biggest lesson Thatcher took from her father was the importance of independent thinking.

"Never do things just because other people do them," he told her once when she had said, "But everyone's doing it."

"Her principles served her well in helping her evaluate any politics or proposals," said Knox. They were the bedrock on which Thatcher built and maintained her political base over her years in public office.

Her standards also had to stand up to the test of debate. As a chemistry student at Oxford, she argued her views in debates at the school's Conservative Association.

Historian John Campbell described how her style of argument helped her persuade and lead.

"She was a very aggressive politician," he said. "She looked for arguments and wanted to win arguments all the time. Most politicians are looking for agreement and trying to be consensual."

Later, Thatcher outlined her ideas in an article in the *Daily Telegraph:* "I was attacked as education secretary for fighting a rear-guard action in defense of 'middle-class interests.' The same accusation is leveled at me now, when I am leading Conservative opposition to the socialist capital transfer tax proposals. Well, if 'middle-class values' include the encouragement of variety and individual choice, the provision of fair incentives and rewards for skill and hard work, the maintenance of effective barriers against the excessive power of the state and a belief in the wide distribution of individual private property, then they are certainly what I am trying to defend."

Patience Moves Mountains

Much of Thatcher's success followed from her good sense of timing — "and her patience," Knox said.

"She was cautious when she knew there was danger of losing," he said. "But then she prepared the grounds for the next time an issue came up."

She had lots of time to do this during two long periods when the Conservative Party was out of power in the U.K.

In such times, major opposition parties in the U.K. form shadow Cabinets. Leading party figures develop plans for different sectors — education, defense, health, finance — as alternatives to the ruling party's positions.

First, Thatcher was the Tory shadow spokeswoman on pensions. She later handled housing and lands and tax. These roles gave her a broad background on national policy.

"If one is to make any serious contribution to the development of policy, one has to master both the big principles and the details," said Thatcher.

As early as 1968, Thatcher was picked to give a yearly Conservative Party Centre lecture. Pollsters had advised the party to choose a subject that would appeal to women voters. Thatcher's "What's Wrong With Government" speech detailed her view that the problem with government was that there was too much of it.

"Partly as a result, I suspect, of the attention I received for the lecture, I was asked to contribute articles on political philosophy to *The Daily Telegraph*," Thatcher said. She used her space in the paper to outline her ideas about the dangers of politics by consensus.

She also cultivated advisers from government, industry, academia and even the press. "She had great ability to inspire loyalty, even among those who were not of her persuasion," Knox said.

Ready In A Crisis

When crises emerged, Thatcher made sure she was ready to confront them, often when others weren't. The Tories lost confidence in their leader, former Prime Minister Edward Heath, after he lost the 1974 election. When the party's favorite for the job, Keith Joseph, bowed out, Thatcher seized the chance. She decided she'd wade right in and stand as candidate for prime minister in the next election.

"It seemed most unlikely that I would win," she said. "But I did think that by entering the race, I would draw in other strong candidates who, even if they did not think like Keith and me, would be open to persuasion about changing the disastrous course on which the party was set."

As party leader, Thatcher expanded the scope of her work. To learn as much as possible for her future role, she visited Britain's allies and many of the world's big trouble spots.

One of Thatcher's greatest talents is her ability to read people. In the shadow Cabinet, "I had the opportunity to demonstrate both to myself and to others that I had the instinct for what ordinary people feel."

Some of this is inborn, she says. But she knew gifts improve with practice. Thatcher, who practically grew up on the campaign trail, had lots of that in the field.

5

Sgt. Alvin York
This Soldier Aimed To Please

When a job needs to be done, the best thing is to stand your ground and do it. So it was that Army Cpl. Alvin York became a hero.

York went on a routine patrol on Oct. 8, 1918, during World War I. He and 15 other American doughboys got orders to take out entrenched German machine gun placements in the Argonne Forest in France.

York was a crack shot. He'd been hunting in the mountains of Tennessee from the time he was small to help feed his family. York was also a religious man who had strong beliefs against killing. He resisted going into the Army until the government inducted him.

Still, when he made a commitment, York honored it. Now he applied all his energy to doing the best job of following orders.

He came back with 132 prisoners in tow.

Although no one knew it, World War I was nearing its end. As the Americans advanced into the heavily defended area, German soldiers killed or wounded half of them, including the sergeant in charge.

York didn't hesitate. He stood and calmly fired at the nearest machine gun placement. Although it may sound like folly to just stand and shoot, it was actually a smart move. York knew his skill with a rifle was his best chance for survival.

York (1887–1964) grew up in the Valley of the Three Forks in the Cumberland Mountains of Tennessee. His father taught him to shoot a rifle at an early age. Every resource was precious, including bullets.

His father scolded him if he missed a shot; it meant not only a lost meal but also a wasted bullet. So the young man practiced aiming with an unloaded gun until he thought he could bag a rabbit with one shot. After that, he usually did.

The young corporal was confident in his shooting skill, realizing that few others shared it. And he knew from hunting that waiting for just the right moment to take a shot was crucial to hitting your target.

So he stood patiently in that open field in France, ignoring the bullets whizzing around him. Then, when a German soldier popped his head up, York shot him.

When it was over, York had killed 25 Germans and, almost single-handedly, captured another 132 — 128 enlisted men and four officers. Armed with a rifle and pistol, he put 35 machine guns out of action.

York knelt on the battlefield after it was over and prayed for the souls of the Americans and Germans killed that day.

Because of York's bravery in that battle, the Yanks were able to retake the Decauville Railroad, a critical site. If the Germans had been able to retreat to the railroad, flee and regroup, the war might have dragged on longer than it did.

The Army promoted York to sergeant and awarded him a host of medals. He said he had so many medals he needed two coats to wear them all.

He received the Distinguished Service Cross, and later the Medal of Honor. He met with President Woodrow Wilson in Paris and the *Saturday Evening Post* ran a story on him.

York returned home a huge hero. People gave him parades and greeted him warmly wherever he went.

Strong Character

York's journey from hillbilly to hero was often difficult. He was born in Fentress County, Tenn. Outside of his war years, he lived there most of his life.

His character was shaped by tough mountain life. He was born in a one-room cabin, the third of 11 children. His father, William York, eked out a living managing a 75-acre farm. His mother took in neighbors' laundry, sometimes in exchange for hand-me-down clothes for her children.

Guns and other hunting weapons were a big part of life in the mountains. York later said one of his earliest memories was hunting snakes and lizards in his yard with a bow and arrow.

Because he could attend school only when his father didn't need him to help with hunting and chores, York made it through only third grade. He understood the importance of education, though, and read on his own when he could.

His father died in 1911 after being kicked by a mule. York had to become the man of the family. It was a big responsibility. Seeking release from the pressure, York started drinking moonshine, gambling and fighting. He got money for his carousing from rifle-shooting contests.

Tough Decisions

Drinking often led to fighting, he found, and "was like to get me in a right smart of trouble." So York turned to the local church to help him stop.

Soon he was deeply involved in church work. Eager to help others as he had been helped, York set up Sunday schools in Fentress County for his own church and others nearby. He took on the added responsibilities of church offices whenever he was needed, conducting services when the pastor was away.

His religious convictions were strong, and when World War I broke out he objected to the war.

"I loved and trusted old Uncle Sam, and I have always believed he did the right thing. But I was worried clean through. I didn't want to go and kill," he later said.

He received a notice to register for the draft in June 1917. He prayed and took long walks in the mountains trying to decide what to do.

Acting on his beliefs, York registered as a conscientious objector. When he was denied, he stayed persistent; he appealed four times. He was turned down each time. Finally, he was inducted into the Army in November 1917.

He finished boot camp with high marks for his shooting skills. Still plagued by doubts about war, he ran to the mountains where he felt at home. He spent all day, that night and part of the next day weighing his decision.

York decided that the U.S. was fighting on the side of right and thus he had to serve his country as a soldier. He was equally confident that God wanted him to fight and would preserve him in battle.

In later years, his advice for those going into battle was "Get determined to get the other fellow before he gets you, keep on thinking about it and with that determination you'll come through."

When World War II broke out, York attempted to re-enlist in the infantry, but age prevented him from doing so. Instead, he signed up with the Signal Corps and traveled the country on bond tours, recruitment drives and camp inspections.

York was buried with full military honors in the Pall Mall cemetery in Tennessee.

6

Bishop's Grit Gave Him Wings

Fighter Ace Was Short On Natural Skill, But Long On Passion

William Avery Bishop's first flight in 1906 was a flop. He and his orange-crate flying machine took off from the veranda roof of his house and landed in a lilac bush.

But 12-year-old Bishop refused to let it be his last. He'd simply learn how to do better.

His willpower to achieve proved formidable. He went on to become Canada's top World War I fighter ace — and one of the best in the world — with 72 victories. He also won the Victoria Cross, the British Empire's highest award for valor. A living legend, he led Canada's pre–World War II campaign to recruit pilots — especially from the U.S.

"Bishop's first crash left him unscathed," says retired Royal Canadian Air Force Group Capt. A.J. Bauer. "But the orange crate was a write-off."

Bishop (1894–1956) grew up in Owen Sound, Ontario, then a bustling port for Great Lakes shipping. Canada in those days was a staunch member of the British Empire. The Union Jack was the national flag.

Bishop also had ties to the U.S. His mother came from Pennsylvania Dutch stock. His father was a lawyer and county registrar who encouraged his children to read. Young Billy eagerly complied.

"Billy was a great reader," said Bauer. "He loved adventure stories and anything about flying."

Billy was 9 when the Wright brothers made their flight. Motivated by their success, he studied everything he could about flying. At 12, he was building aircraft models that a local shopkeeper displayed.

Taking Flight

Bishop followed in his older brother's footsteps and entered the Royal Military College — the Canadian West Point — in 1911.

While fascinated by flight, the younger Bishop was less than enthusiastic about his studies. He barely muddled through college. Then the start of war in 1914 sent senior cadets into service early, and Bishop was among them.

He sailed on a cattle ship from Canada to England in June 1915. Hating the mud and horse manure of the army camp, Bishop saw a British Royal Flying Corps plane land and take off. "Flying," he later wrote, is "the only way to fight a war — up there above the mud and the mist in the everlasting sunshine."

Bishop turned his sights on the Royal Flying Corps. Unfortunately for him, they already had plenty of pilots. Determined to get in anyway, he signed on as an observer.

It was, he figured, a foot in the door. Less than a year later, in May 1916, he applied for pilot training.

Bishop had a decided lack of natural talent. All too often, his landings were like his childhood orange-crate experiment.

But he had drive. He resolved he'd improve, and he spent hours outside of flight training practicing.

Finally, he won his wings and began combat duty in France in March 1917. He flew a Nieuport Scout, a small biplane with a rotary engine and a machine gun above the top wing.

The Nieuport required a deft hand. Bishop had a heavy hand — and foot. On March 24, 1917, another crash landing threatened to send him back to flight school.

So the next day, he focused on redeeming himself. He led an attack of four Nieuports on three German planes. So keen was he on winning, he chased one German plane through a 9,000-foot dive, sending it right into the ground.

That feat kept him in the war. His determination to stay on top ensured that more victories followed.

In World War I, an ace could adopt "colors" to identify himself to the enemy. Germany's Red Baron did it. Bishop also wanted to set himself apart, so he trimmed his Nieuport in bright blue.

It wasn't enough for Bishop to win dogfights; he also wanted to find a better method of fighting in the air. So he experimented with tactics, pioneering one called deflection.

As a moving object, a plane had a definite path, as did bullets. If he aimed right at a plane, the aircraft would've moved forward by the time his bullet arrived and the shot would've been useless. So Bishop shot ahead of a plane to hit it.

Pajama Party

When it came to solo attacks, Bishop's courage knew few bounds. One such attack earned him the Victoria Cross, Britain's highest honor.

On June 2, 1917, in rain and mist, Bishop took off at 3:57 a.m. He wore pajamas under his flying suit.

Lost in the murk, he dropped below the clouds and found a German airfield. Seven aircraft sat ready, their engines running.

Bishop acted fast. Through a hail of groundfire, he strafed the planes. As he turned to strafe again, one German lifted off. Bishop got him.

He scared a second into a tree. Two more German planes took off in opposite directions.

Bishop took them on. He got one. The second fled.

Then Bishop's gun jammed. Knowing that sometimes it's better to live and fight another day, he tossed it overboard and fled to British lines.

Unarmed and alone, he had to outrun four German planes. He dived at full power to friendly territory, through anti-aircraft fire.

The Royal Flying Corps' commander called Bishop's mission "the greatest single show of the war."

When it came to personnel, Bishop believed in hiring the best and forming a tight team. Ordered to form a new squadron in March 1918, he persuaded gutsy pilots from the U.S., New Zealand, Canada and Britain to join him.

In June 1918, he got orders to leave the war to create a Canadian Flying Corps. Bound to leave his mark, he shot down five more enemy planes during his last flight.

As the war ended, Lt. Col. Bishop had 72 confirmed victories. The Red Baron had 80. A French pilot had 75.

Bishop launched a postwar air charter firm in Ontario. It flopped. Returning to Britain, he built a new business career. The crash of 1929 wiped him out.

Unbowed, he took a job with McColl Frontenac Oil Co. This time he thrived, but war loomed again.

Bishop had a deep sense of honor, says his son, Arthur Bishop, a historian who wrote his father's story in "The Courage of the Early Morning."

"My dad wouldn't put up with any nonsense," Bishop said in a recent interview. "He was adamant about what he thought was right and wrong."

And Bishop thought the rise of Nazi Germany was wrong. It was time to once more devote himself to his country.

The Canadian government promoted Bishop to honorary RCAF air vice marshal in 1936 and air marshal in 1938. His job? To build a modern air force.

Again, he looked for the best pilots. He trekked across America, giving rousing speeches and lobbying talented fliers to persuade them to join the RCAF.

Ill health and exhaustion forced him to step down in 1944. He died in his sleep at his Palm Beach, Fla., vacation home 12 years later.

7

Calvin Coolidge

Quiet President Worked For Limited Government

For Calvin Coolidge, life was all about the bottom line. But not just the financial bottom line. His bottom line included personal integrity and frugal, limited government.

That approach made Coolidge, the 30th president, one of the nation's most successful. Under his leadership, America enjoyed peace and tremendous prosperity.

Coolidge (1872–1933) was born in Plymouth Notch, Vt. Growing up on a farm, he was hard at work from an early age, tapping maple trees, shearing sheep, shucking corn and picking apples.

While he was a small boy who suffered from asthma, he didn't complain about the hard labor. He knew that without work his family wouldn't eat or enjoy any other comforts. In fact, he embraced it.

In 1891, Coolidge entered Amherst College in Massachusetts. The painfully shy Coolidge, known as "Silent Cal," struggled to make friends. He knew his shyness was a barrier to happiness and success.

So he set out to tackle the problem. He forced himself to speak to strangers and enter debates. His first attempts were difficult, but he kept practicing and improved with effort.

As he grew more comfortable, people discovered that he had a dry wit. The awkward farm boy became popular, even joining a fraternity in his senior year.

The shyness never really left him. Even late in life he confessed that when meeting a stranger he'd panic and want to flee the room. But he repeatedly directed himself to fight the urge.

Dogged Persistence

"Nothing in the world can take the place of persistence," Coolidge later wrote. "Talent will not; nothing is more common than unsuccessful men with talent. Genius will not; unrewarded genius is almost a proverb. Education will not; the world is full of educated derelicts. Persistence and determination are omnipotent."

After graduating from Amherst, Coolidge decided his passion lay in the law. So he took a job as a clerk at a law firm in Northampton, Mass. At night, he studied.

In 1898, Coolidge passed the bar and started his own law practice. He also won election to the city council. The post was unpaid, but Coolidge knew it would bring him in contact with people who could help his law practice and political career.

Coolidge was fond of saying a long journey consists of many small steps. His rise in politics proved that. Over the next decade, he went from the city council to city solicitor to the state House of Representatives.

"Each new office was a rung on the ladder," said Robert Ferrell, author of "The Presidency of Calvin Coolidge."

In 1909, the voters of Northampton elected Coolidge mayor. Devoted to efficiency, he campaigned on a platform of frugal but effective government.

Having achieved success in his hometown, Coolidge set his sights on bigger goals. After his second term as mayor, he won a seat in the state Senate.

Coolidge built a reputation for honesty and hard work by coming early, staying late and keeping his word. In 1914, his peers elected him president of the Senate.

After serving two terms as Senate president, Coolidge again set his eyes on a larger prize. In 1916, he crisscrossed the state, campaigning for the position of lieutenant governor. He won that office and served three terms. Then he decided it was again time to build on his success and run for governor. He won.

The defining moment of Coolidge's term in office was the Boston police strike of 1919. Three-quarters of the city's police force walked out because of low pay and poor working conditions. Coolidge sympathized with their plight.

But when riots broke out, Coolidge resolved to do what was necessary to end the violence — he called out the National Guard.

"There is no right to strike against the public safety by anybody, anywhere, any time!" he said.

His stand brought him national attention. The Republican Party named Coolidge its vice presidential candidate for Warren Harding in 1920.

The two were elected. On Aug. 2, 1923, a heart attack felled Harding, and Coolidge became president.

As he took office, the corruption of Harding's administration began to spill into public view. The Teapot Dome scandal, in which top officials took bribes to open up federal lands for oil drilling, was Coolidge's first real test.

Stuck To Principles

Interior Secretary Albert Fall was convicted of taking bribes. Several other officials resigned in disgrace.

Throughout the scandal, Coolidge stuck to his principles and insisted the truth had to come out. He protected no one. As a result, none of the scandals touched him.

In 1924, he easily won election on his own. Happily incorporating others' good ideas, he continued the good part of Harding's administration — tax cuts and keeping spending in check. As a result, the economy and stock market soared.

In 1927, he stunned the nation by announcing he wouldn't run for re-election the next year. He was immensely popular and likely would've won. But Coolidge knew when it was time to call it a day; friends said the joy of being president had left him when his son Calvin Jr. died three years earlier.

8

President Theodore Roosevelt
He Relied On Persistence To Overcome Obstacles

Theodore Roosevelt was born with a quick mind and a courageous spirit. Then there was his body — that required some work.

As a boy he was small and weak. His eyesight was bad, and he suffered from asthma.

At the age of 10, his father told him, "You have the mind but you have not the body. You must make the body."

Roosevelt (1858–1919) realized that his father had a point — and he wanted to be strong on all fronts. Determined to overcome his weakness, he focused all his efforts on pushing his physical limits.

In a gym that his father built for him, Roosevelt lifted weights and practiced gymnastics daily. To make sure he developed all his muscles equally, he also rode horseback, swam, hiked and studied wrestling, boxing and judo.

The exercise paid off, and Roosevelt found himself hale and hearty. His asthma faded, and he learned the lesson that he could take charge of a situation and mold it to his specifications.

Sound Of Body And Mind

But the development of Roosevelt's physique didn't come at the expense of the mind. When his asthma confined him to his bed as a boy, "T.R.," as he liked to be called, developed a love of reading. He read as often as he could even after his asthma had healed. And that stayed with him his entire life.

Roosevelt, born in New York, decided that to stay on his toes and remain sharp in all areas he needed to keep challenging himself. So he headed west, seeking credibility as a rancher in the badlands of South Dakota. He read everything he could about ranching and hired people who could teach him about cattle.

Whenever he was faced with a problem, Roosevelt confronted it directly. Several times he was challenged to fistfights by men who were much larger than he. Yet he didn't back down — he fought and won. During the Spanish-American War, he led his Rough Riders cavalry unit straight up San Juan Hill despite his fear that he or his men might be wounded.

Roosevelt refused to let anything stand in the way of what he felt was his duty. Take the time he was shot in the chest just before a speech during a presidential campaign in 1912. Roosevelt insisted on giving the speech before treating the wound.

"I have a message to deliver," he said, "and I will deliver it as long as there is life in my body."

Roosevelt had tremendous energy. He didn't want to waste a moment. Often called the most dynamic U.S. president, he slept just four or five hours a night. While his family slept, Roosevelt used the late-night and early morning hours to read, catch up on paperwork or study.

That determination to get as much out of life as possible often left others feeling dizzy. Writer Rudyard Kipling once remarked, "I curled up in the seat opposite, and listened and wondered, until the universe seemed to be spinning around and Theodore was the spinner."

A bookworm cowboy, Roosevelt was a study in contrasts, historians say. An avid hunter, he was known as a "military hawk who often advocated war for the sake of war," according to biographer Henry Pringle. "He admired soldierly virtues such as discipline and wanted to restore the fighting edge to the American spirit," said Richard Hofstadter in "The American Political Tradition."

Shortly after his famous storming of San Juan, where some of his men died, he reportedly called the charge great fun. He declared the U.S. the "policeman of the Western Hemisphere," and he followed the motto, "Speak softly and carry a big stick."

Yet he was dedicated to peaceful solutions when he felt they were practical. He won the Nobel Peace Prize in 1906 for mediating between Japan and Russia a year earlier and staving off further conflict between the two countries.

Long-Term Vision

Roosevelt knew that all things have limits — such as the natural resources that exist in the U.S. While he believed that they existed to be used by humans, he realized that they had to be treated carefully so they would last.

"We are prone to speak of the resources of this country as inexhaustible; that is not so," he said in 1907.

He examined the open spaces left throughout the country. He spoke to a number of forestry experts and open-space advocates, especially Sierra Club founder John Muir.

As a result, Roosevelt agreed to legally protect more than 150 million acres of wilderness, the most dramatic act of preservation of any president until that point.

Roosevelt also used the presidency to give voice to the voiceless.

He championed the rights of laborers and fought against what he saw as robber barons, even when it meant taking on J.P. Morgan and the Northern Securities Co.

He didn't kowtow to critics. When he wanted to learn more about black educator Booker T. Washington and his projects, Roosevelt invited him to the White House. Southern Democrats were enraged: Roosevelt ignored them, and the meeting went on as planned.

Roosevelt wouldn't allow himself to be pigeonholed. When he first went to the Dakotas, many of the ranchers were quick to dismiss the Harvard graduate as a four-eyed dude.

He ignored their taunts and let his actions speak for themselves. During cattle drives, he cut through the cattle as well as any cowboy. He spent as much time in the saddle as his humblest ranch hand. Soon, the taunts died away.

Roosevelt went into politics because he felt strongly that he had a duty to serve the public. He was honest, and he expected others to behave in the same fashion.

When he discovered they weren't, he acted swiftly. After he became commissioner of the New York Police Department, Roosevelt railed against the status quo by weeding corruption and incompetence from the force.

He'd make late-night patrols through the streets of New York, haranguing officers who were drinking or taking up with women.

Even as the youngest president ever — he was 42 when William McKinley's assassination thrust Vice President Roosevelt into chiefdom — he never ducked a fight.

He sought to have "In God We Trust" removed from U.S. coins, calling it unconstitutional — a fight he didn't win. He supported a revolt in Panama that paved the way to the building of the Panama Canal — a fight he did win.

Roosevelt knew the importance of balance in his life. In addition to his near-constant reading and lecturing, he stayed physically active until very near his death. He left for a safari in Africa after his presidency and led an expedition into the Amazon in 1914.

He once said he promised himself as a youth that he would live his life up to the hilt until 60. He did just that.

9

Sam Houston

His Disciplined Strategy
Secured Texas For The Nation

When he was 14 years old, his father died. At 16, he ran away from home. He made time for only one year of school.

By the time he was a young man, he'd earned a reputation as a carouser and a drunk.

But Samuel Houston knew hard work could dig him out of his moral ditch. Within a few short years, he'd grown into a visionary whose actions were pivotal to America's expansion in the West.

He led the military victory that sealed Texas' independence from Mexico, and then he championed the Lone Star Republic's entry to the U.S.

Born near Lexington, Va., Houston became the first president of the Republic of Texas and later served a separate second term. He also served that state as a U.S. senator, congressman and governor. Earlier he'd served as a congressman and governor of Tennessee.

Houston (1793–1863) held more military and public offices than anyone else in American history, according to historian James McPherson.

Houston was seen as a potential candidate for U.S. president as early as age 35, Frank Krystyniak wrote at the Sam Houston State University Web site. And if he'd become president in 1856 or 1860, his political savvy might have prevented the Civil War, wrote historian John Hoyt Williams.

Never Stopped Learning

To reverse his bleak, early prospects, Houston began by improving his mind. Despite his lack of formal instruction, in his late teens he read Homer's "Iliad" so often that he memorized most of its 24 books.

And he never stopped learning. In the Army, Houston stuffed into his knapsack the Bible, Shakespeare's works and such books as "Robinson Crusoe."

He also was honest enough to see his own limitations. When he ran away from home, he settled in with a band of 300 Cherokee Indians, figuring he needed a community to survive. He did this at a time when most American Anglos despised American Indians, wrote biographer Marquis James. In turn, Chief Oo-loo-te-ka raised Houston like a son, giving him valuable guidance. Houston soaked up information on wildlife, trapping and agriculture. He'd later find it all invaluable when talking with frontier families.

After military service, Houston went to Nashville, Tenn. Deciding that law was a good fit, he dove into and completed an 18-month law school course in six months.

He saw politics as a way to make changes, and he served two terms in Congress before being elected governor of Tennessee. But in 1829 at age 35 he divorced his 18-year-old wife after three months of marriage. Historians speculate that the causes were his drunkenness and jealousy toward a former rival.

Houston was forced to resign as governor. Within a few years, drinking cost him his second marriage.

Finally recognizing that he had a problem, Houston gave up drinking with his third marriage, to Margaret Lea in 1840.

As he matured, Houston often relied on humor — especially about himself — when talking with others. He knew that making fun of his foibles made others feel more at ease around him. When a friend asked if all his sins had been washed away by his church baptism in a local creek as an adult, Houston said he felt "sorry for the fish if they were," according to biographer Marshall De Bruhl.

Houston sought challenges. In 1832, Houston joined American settlers who moved into Texas, which was a province of Mexico. Tension with the Mexican government led to war in 1836. With his public service record and having fought in the War of 1812, Houston was made commander of rebel forces.

He analyzed his moves carefully before making them. When Mexicans massacred the Alamo garrison 70 miles away, Houston's enraged soldiers demanded to counterattack immediately. Instead, Houston ordered a retreat.

His force almost mutinied. But Houston's assessment of the situation told him it was his only hope for eventual victory.

Mexican Gen. Santa Anna had 5,500 crack troops under his command. Houston had just 400 men, largely untrained and undisciplined. A similarly passionate, outgunned force of 189 men had ignored Houston's order to evacuate the Alamo. Santa Anna's soldiers had killed them and burned their bodies.

Houston remembered the price he once paid for being hotheaded. He was a young officer under the legendary Gen. Andrew Jackson in the War of 1812. In the Battle of Horseshoe Bend he fought recklessly and barely survived three wounds.

So now, rather than charge the stronger Mexicans, he marched his army away, toward Louisiana.

Houston was innovative. He ordered his men to light campfires to fool enemy scouts into thinking he was bivouacking. But he kept his men on the move.

He recruited soldiers along the way, building his force to 900. In swampland north of the Brazos River, he ran drills and waited for Santa Anna to make a mistake.

Houston got his wish when the Mexican dictator-general divided his army. Santa Anna sent part of his force to pursue Texas government officials and kept after Houston with a smaller force. He found Houston at the San Jacinto River.

Houston knew that strategy would help his men survive. So when the Mexicans prepared for the customary dawn attack on April 21, 1836, Houston held his men back. Exhausted by their own forced march, Santa Anna's men settled in for the afternoon siesta.

Relying on the element of surprise, Houston deployed infantry and cavalry on three sides. He ordered his men to advance silently. It was 4:30 p.m., an unheard of hour for attack.

In the ferocious fight that ensued, Houston had two horses shot out from under him. A musket ball mashed his ankle.

But in just 18 minutes, half of Santa Anna's 1,250-man force lay dead. Houston lost six men, with 13 wounded.

Taken prisoner, Santa Anna ordered the rest of his army — only 50 miles away — home.

Texas was set free.

Houston worked tirelessly to make his dream of building a democratic nation a reality. He followed the examples of his mentor in nationalism, the charismatic Jackson, and his own father, who'd fought in the Revolution. He lobbied for Texas' annexation as a state.

United It Stands

A slave owner, Houston was flawed. But knowing that strength comes from unity, he worked hard to preserve the Union by steering the South away from secession. Eight years before Abraham Lincoln famously used the biblical allusion, Sam Houston warned other Southern legislators that, "A nation divided against itself cannot stand," according to historian Randolph Campbell.

Houston stuck by his fierce nationalism no matter the cost. When secession came, he was alone among Southern governors in refusing to take an oath of allegiance to the Confederacy even though it meant he was forced from office.

Together, the U.S. could do great things, Houston predicted.

"A lot of people had sight," Houston's great-great-granddaughter Margaret Rost told the *Houston Chronicle* last year. "But few had (Houston's) vision."

PART 2

Building Trust With Integrity

Loyalty is frequently only considered as faithfulness from the bottom up. It has another and equally important application that is from the top down. One of the most frequently noted characteristics of the great who remained great is . . . loyalty to their subordinates.

— GENERAL GEORGE S. PATTON (FROM "ON WAR AND LEADERSHIP" BY OWEN CONNELLY)

10

President
Harry S. Truman
He Gave His All

Harry Truman discovered there comes a time in every man's life when he simply has to stand up and take charge.

That moment arrived for Truman in 1917, when he was a 33-year-old commander of a rowdy Army Reserve artillery battery that was soon to be shipped off to the front lines in France to fight in World War I.

Previous captains had failed to corral this notorious wild bunch. Indeed, during his first night in charge his men broke into a barracks brawl. The next morning, Truman pinned up a list of all the officers he had stripped of their rank. He then called all his noncommissioned officers to a meeting.

"I didn't come over here to get along with you," Truman (1884–1972) said to the assembled noncoms. "You've got to get along with me. And if there are any of you who can't, speak up right now and I'll bust you right back now." No one spoke up.

Earning Respect

From this take-charge opening salvo, and throughout their 1918 campaign in France, Truman's men understood who was in charge. The refined Missouri moralist who loved classical music and Europe's great art masters would, over time, gain the respect and admiration of these earthy soldiers. By the time of Germany's surrender, Truman's battalion was recognized as one of the best fighting units in the regiment.

Through integrity and a strong work ethic, this unlikely leader propelled his way up the rungs of power and onto the world stage. He served as U.S. senator from 1935 to 1945, vice president in 1945, then as the 33rd president from the death of Franklin Roosevelt in 1945 to 1953. He helped end World War II, established a containment policy against the Soviet Union, helped create the Marshall Plan to save Europe in 1948 and helped create the North Atlantic Treaty Organization in 1949. He also ordered the Berlin Airlift in 1948 and 1949, and initiated U.S. engagement in Korea in 1950.

Today he is recognized as one of the top presidents. Columnist George F. Will has called Truman the last great leader the nation has had.

Truman believed in shouldering responsibility, according to Ken Hechler. Hechler was a Princeton University political science professor in 1949 when he was recruited to the Truman White House to write the president's speeches. Hechler recalled in a recent interview how the president, whose Oval Office desk held the sign "The Buck Stops Here," called a staff meeting to announce a news conference. Gen. Douglas MacArthur was being relieved of his command.

One of the junior staffers stood up and told the president he should say that this move came with the unanimous support of the joint chiefs.

The way Hechler remembers it, Truman responded, "Son, history will probably record exactly what you've said. But tonight this is something I must take responsibility for personally without passing the buck to anyone else."

There was silence in the room. "You could almost hear the Liberty Bell ring in the background," said Hechler, who draws on his six years in the White House and 18 years as a congressman from West Virginia to teach a course on Truman at Marshall University.

Hechler says Truman created intense loyalty among his staff by making it feel genuinely cared for. That included everyone. "The cooks, the ushers, the electricians, Truman knew them all and asked them about their families," Hechler said.

"I remember one day one of the cooks told me that Truman was the first president since Calvin Coolidge to visit the kitchen. He said, 'Coolidge visited the kitchen because he wanted to check on whether people were stealing food, but Truman came to compliment them (on doing) a good job.'"

Truman scholar Randy Sowell, archivist for the Harry S. Truman Library in Independence, Mo., says it was Truman's strong sense of ethics and diligence that earned him the respect of fellow senators after he joined them in 1935.

In addition to following his parents' examples, Truman learned from history's finest.

"Reading history, to me, was far more than a romantic adventure," Truman said. "It was solid instruction and wise teaching which I somehow felt that I wanted and needed."

Despite his voracious reading, Truman in no way thought he knew it all. Sowell says when Truman entered the Senate, it was under a cloud of uncertainty whether he had what it took.

But he figured hard work would aid him. And he took steps to master each project that came his way.

He went to work so early each morning that by midafternoon staffers said he needed another shave. According to David McCullough's biography, "Truman," he was the first senator to receive his own passkey for early morning building access.

It was Sen. Truman's scrupulous attention to detail that earned him a reputation for getting things done right. Assigned to the Interstate Commerce Committee that was looking into railroad financing, Truman attended every meeting, where it was said he spoke rarely and listened much.

He toted back from the Library of Congress some 50 books on railroad history and management. "I'm going to be better informed on the transportation problem than anyone here," Truman said.

Authority From Knowledge

This desire to master the subject led to Truman being perceived as a man of authority who could be counted on. He led the committee that examined the U.S. effort in World War II and looked at issues such as war manufacturing, shipping losses and gasoline rationing.

Truman's simple premise for the committee's role was not to make a name for itself or carry on a witch hunt. The members were to get the facts. "There is no substitute for facts," Truman told them. "Give the work all you've got."

The results were impressive. The committee exposed defective production of airplane engines and steel and was able to steer the Defense Department to create shallow-water landing vehicles. Truman's efforts were recognized nationally, and he found himself on the March 8, 1943, cover of *Time* magazine. The magazine called him scrupulously honest, his only vice being an occasional game of poker.

But Hechler argues you have to admire the man's sheer persistence in the way he courted his wife. "She wouldn't even look at him in high school," Hechler said. "He fell in love with her when they were 5 or 6 years old in Sunday school and there was only one woman in his life. He persisted. This was a quality he possessed. The ability to look at a problem and not be discouraged by the obstacles."

"I've had a few setbacks in my life," Truman said, "but I never gave up."

11

Gen. George S. Patton
He Led With Boldness And Clear Intentions

America was about to enter World War II, and Gen. George S. Patton wanted his junior officers to have a clear picture of what he expected of them.

He gathered his men around a dining room table, at the center of which lay a limp noodle on a plate.

Patton began to push the noodle. It wiggled but scarcely moved.

Then, he grabbed one end and in a single motion pulled it across the plate. "Gentlemen," he said, looking at them, "you don't push . . . you lead."

That ability to clearly convey his intentions made Patton (1885–1945) one of the most masterful leaders in U.S. military history.

He played key roles in Allied victories by leading American tank troops across Europe and North Africa. Dwight D. Eisenhower called him the best Allied general in Europe.

Perhaps because he was dyslexic, Patton understood the importance of careful instruction. In fact, wrote historian Roger Nye, Patton trained "his officers to be trainers." It was always Patton's style to teach, whether by explaining, harassing, cajoling or cursing.

Leadership Quality

He wasn't a born leader. In fact, as a child, he was shy and fragile-looking. His family labeled him "delicate."

An aunt decided to toughen him up by telling him about the great battles in the Bible and classical mythology and history. His father joined in with stories about relatives who'd fought in the Civil War.

Hour after hour, young Patton sat spellbound. Learning disability or not, he realized, he could become great by developing the character of a warrior.

Throughout his life, he studied the profiles and strategies of military heroes through the ages. And while still a youth, he listed the qualities he'd foster. In addition to becoming tactically aggressive, he decided to develop:

- Strength of character
- Steadiness of purpose
- Acceptance of responsibility
- Energy, good health and strength

Patton started out by acting the part.

"He began to affect personality traits," wrote Carlo d'Este in "Patton: A Genius for War," "in short, to reinvent himself in the guise of a rugged, macho male."

He enrolled in the Virginia Military Institute and the U.S. Military Academy at West Point.

Testing himself, he took chances that nearly cost him his life. But they proved he could develop the mettle he wanted.

For example, while marking targets during rifle practice at West Point, he stood up and "faced the firing line, unflinching, as bullets angrily splattered around him," d'Este wrote.

Unless forced to stop, he always acted boldly. He adopted the motto of Frederick the Great, "L'audace, l'audace, toujours l'audace" — "audacity, audacity, always audacity."

Even after he became general, Patton spent hours in front of the mirror practicing his "war face," a scowl he wore when addressing his men.

Patton put great effort into learning to communicate clearly. He directed himself to reduce his thoughts to as few words as possible. In doing so, he became a powerful communicator.

As a general, his orders were clear and rarely exceeded a single page. Quick to use the power of a clear picture, he'd often sketch a map on the back.

Morale Builder

Patton was sensitive to his men's sense of their own worth. Whenever he gave an order, he made certain not to blunt their initiative.

"Never tell people how to do things," he wrote. "Tell them what to do, and they will surprise you with their ingenuity."

Still, Patton insisted on discipline so strict that even other generals thought him a martinet.

"Lack of discipline at play means the loss of a few yards," he told his men. "Lack of discipline in war means death, or defeat, which is worse than death."

He'd assess a soldier's level of discipline by his appearance — even in combat. Many of his tank troopers not only were clean-shaven at all times, but they also wore ties.

If Patton demanded much of his men, he also praised them when they delivered.

He thought that great courage or initiative in battle should be promptly rewarded with medals and other honors. If possible, he gave the awards himself. And he always gave credit for his victories to his men.

Take how he described the Battle of the Bulge. The battle, waged in the Ardennes plateau, was a huge, unexpected effort by the Germans to push back the Allies.

Panic reigned through much of the Allied forces. But Patton saw the battle as an opportunity to direct a killing blow at the Germans. He made plans to turn his troops, which had been heading east, northward to attack the German flank.

The years of training his officers and men to be as capable as he paid off.

"Only a commander with exceptional confidence in his subordinate commanders and in the professional skill of his fighting divisions could dare risk such a venture," d'Este wrote.

In less than two days, Patton's forces were turning the Germans back. Talking to reporters, the general gave full credit to his men.

"We hit the sons of bitches on the flank and stopped them cold. Now that may sound like George Patton is a great genius. Actually he had damned little to do with it. All he did was give orders."

12

Statesman Yitzhak Rabin
His Push For Peace Made Him
A World Figure

"We should not let the land flowing with milk and honey become the land flowing with blood and tears."

That commitment to peace helped Yitzhak Rabin become a world figure in the decades he served Israel. As chief of staff of the army, ambassador to the U.S. and two-time prime minister, Rabin pushed constantly for peace in the Middle East.

Born in Jerusalem to parents who had moved to Palestine from the U.S., Rabin (1922–95) learned about public service early on. His parents were active in Jewish military and political organizations.

In his book "The Rabin Memoirs," he said, "Our home was permeated with a sense of mission. Work was considered a value in itself."

That included schoolwork. Rabin attended primary school in Tel Aviv, and in 1940, he graduated with honors from Kedoorie Agricultural College in Lower Galilee.

But his parents' message of activism lingered, and when World War II broke out, he turned down a scholarship to the University of California at Berkeley in order to join a youth training group north of Haifa. He became an active member of the Haganah, the independent Jewish military.

Eager to make a difference, he was one of the first to volunteer in 1941 for the Palmach, the commando unit of the Jewish Defense Forces, and he fought against the Vichy French in Syria and Lebanon. He quickly achieved commander status and served in the Palmach and in the Israeli army for 27 years.

Tactical Training

In the Palmach, Rabin learned to be resourceful. He figured out schedules that would distribute limited supplies most evenly. If an item ran out, Rabin found a substitute.

To provide the best example, Rabin stayed disciplined. He rose early, worked passionately and studied military training manuals at night.

Once done reading, Rabin would get inventive with his own training doctrine. He pushed soldiers to be as physically fit as possible.

He would do anything he expected them to do. His leadership style became known by his command, "Follow me."

After Israel became an independent nation in 1948 and was attacked by its Arab neighbors, Rabin led the defense of Jerusalem and fought in the Negev.

In 1949, Rabin had his first taste of peace negotiations at the end of Israel's War of Independence when he was a member of the Israeli delegation. The experience inspired him.

Rabin was appointed chief of the general staff in 1962 and promoted to the rank of lieutenant general. His strategy of swift mobilization, superior airpower and destruction of enemy aircraft on the ground helped Israel win the Six-Day War in 1967.

After retiring from the army in 1968, Rabin was appointed ambassador to the U.S. Considering U.S. support of supreme importance, he worked to foster solid ties with America. He also worked on a peace process with the Arab states. He went out of his way to write personal letters to other diplomats. He asked for face-to-face meetings with as many business and political leaders as he could.

His hard work paid off. U.S. military aid to Israel increased dramatically.

Rabin returned to Jerusalem in 1973 after five years as ambassador. Seeing that Israel's strength lay in its relationships, he decided to delve further into politics. He ran on Israel's Labor ticket and got elected to the Knesset, the Israeli parliament.

Throwing himself into his new job, Rabin spent nearly all his days and nights consensus building. By March 1974, he was appointed minister of labor in the government formed by Golda Meir.

His skill at forging relationships won him the people's confidence. The Knesset voted for Rabin to succeed Meir as prime minister in 1974. His first term lasted until 1977.

Constant Improvement

Rabin, the first native-born prime minister, sought to improve relations abroad, boost the Israeli economy, work on social issues and strengthen the military.

He became known for his undeviating and sometimes blunt leadership style. He wasn't afraid of hard work. He believed in personal contact instead of relying on the traditional hierarchy and chain of command.

In 1975, Rabin signed an interim agreement with Egypt with mediation from the U.S. that stated Israel would withdraw forces from the Suez Canal area in return for free passage of Israeli shipping through the canal.

As a result of this agreement, the first Memorandum of Understanding was signed between the government of Israel and the U.S., after which the U.S. pledged continued support for Israel in the international arena.

Rabin was willing to take chances to hold true to his beliefs, even in the face of danger. In June 1976, Palestinian terrorists hijacked Air France passengers to Uganda. Refusing to negotiate with the terrorists, Rabin ordered the Entebbe Operation. The Israeli army swiftly reached deep into Uganda, rescuing the hostages and delivering them safely to Israel.

Rabin knew when to put aside personal differences. Working closely with his longtime rival, Israeli Foreign Minister Shimon Peres, Rabin masterminded a plan that outlined the cooperation of Israel and the Palestinians in stages. This plan, called the Oslo Agreement, has served as the basis for peacemaking efforts, including the Camp David Accords.

In May 1989, the Israeli government adopted his plan. Rabin, then defense minister, was able to help put it into action when he served his second term as prime minister, starting in 1992.

On Sept. 13, 1993, Rabin and Palestine Liberation Organization Chairman Yasser Arafat signed the Declaration of Principles in Washington, D.C., outlining the proposed interim self-government arrangements. The "Gaza Jericho First" agreement, signed in Cairo, Egypt, on May 4, 1994, addressed the first stage of the Declaration of Principles.

Following the agreement with the Palestinians, Rabin received the 1994 Nobel Peace Prize together with Peres and Arafat.

A critical part of the new Middle East peace process was the Israel-Jordan peace treaty, signed with King Hussein of Jordan in October 1994. This agreement encouraged the development of ties between Israel and Arab countries in North Africa and the Persian Gulf.

Rabin's peace efforts with the Palestinians garnered him the hatred of some.

On Nov. 4, 1995, Yitzhak Rabin was assassinated by Jewish student extremist Yigal Amir in central Tel Aviv after attending a peace rally.

13

Confederate Gen. Robert E. Lee

Troops Rallied 'Round His Principled Leadership

Journalists called him "Granny Lee" and "Evacuating Lee." He was overcareful, fearful and unfit, they declared. All this because Gen. Robert E. Lee forced Southern troops to fight from behind barricades starting in 1862.

Lee's wife, Mary, was outraged at the criticism. She wanted to write harsh letters to the newspapers. Lee asked her to ignore the insults.

He said it was better to "go steadily in the discharge of duty to the best of our ability, leaving all else to the calmer judgment of the future and to a kinder Providence."

The Virginia native proved right. Lee (1807–70) is regarded as one of the top military leaders of all time. Dwight Eisenhower lauded Lee for his "selfless dedication to duty." Winston Churchill called Lee "one of the noblest Americans who ever lived, and one of the greatest captains known to the annals of war."

How did he do it? First of all, Lee led by example.

When he took command of Confederate forces in 1862, he received an army of beaten-down troops from Gen. Joseph Johnston. But Lee didn't bully his men into shape.

Instead, Lee rose daily at 3 a.m. He'd then ride the lines all day. At age 54, Lee "possibly surpassed every other American soldier of his time in his ability to stay on his feet or in the saddle day after day," said Charles Roland, author of "Reflections on Lee: A Historian's Assessment."

Superb Physical Condition

Lee trained himself to be in top physical shape. Before the war, he'd ridden 10 miles a day, hiked, rowed, high jumped and swum.

He gave orders calmly and quietly. He also urged his men to come to him with problems. "His staff was sometimes taken aback by this," said Col. James Speicher, director of nonresident studies at the U.S. Army's Command and General Staff College in Fort Leavenworth, Kan.

At night, after his staff went to bed, Lee stayed up in the command tent and pored over maps by candlelight. "Does he never sleep?" puzzled one of his majors.

Lee even led his troops months after suffering what might've been a heart attack. Once, overcome by severe stomach pains, he guided his army from the back of an ambulance.

Lee also insisted upon living as humbly as his troops did.

"He was able to elicit extraordinary achievements from his men," said Professor Joseph Glatthaar of the University of Houston, author of "The March to the Sea and Beyond." When Lee's soldiers put their lives on the line during battle, some were known to say later, "I did it for Marse Robert."

At first, Lee's troops were leery of his military abilities. Lee ordered them to build barricades — called *breastworks* — and fight from behind them. It seemed strange to his men to do this rather than face off with the Northern forces.

"His soldiers were initially offended by this," Speicher said. "They believed that gentlemen should not hide behind piles of dirt to fight.

"But Lee was ahead of his time. He knew the value of defensive works. So, soon his soldiers found out that this strategy enabled them to balance out the North's superior strength and numbers," Speicher said.

Lee refused to let his troops pillage, even though Union foes brutally sacked his native state. Northern Gen. John Pope ordered a "pillaging campaign," during which his troops shot colts, horses, mules and oxen, and destroyed Virginians' crops.

But Lee reminded his troops, "It must be remembered that we make war only on armed men, and that we cannot take vengeance for the wrongs our people have suffered without lowering ourselves." Foragers caught red-handed were forced to pay for what they took.

Lee's strong religious faith gave him peace during war. The blade of his sword bore the French inscription, "Aide toi et Dieu t'aidera" "Help yourself, and God will help you."

Lee was also pragmatic. He taught himself to make the best of his fate, whatever it might be.

He passed on his realism to his family, even urging his son to avoid reading fiction.

Novels, Lee said, "paint beauty more charming than nature and describe happiness that never exists. They will teach him . . . to despise the little good that is granted us in this world and to expect more than is given."

By early April 1865, Lee knew his starving army couldn't hold off the Northern forces. Hoping to spare his men further suffering, Lee surrendered to Gen. Ulysses S. Grant on April 9, 1865.

Keeping The Horses

In a final show of concern for soldiers in his care, Lee asked Grant to allow the Confederate troops to keep their horses for civilian work. Grant agreed and also issued food for the ex-soldiers, according to Jack Kavanagh and Eugene C. Murdoch, authors of "Robert E. Lee: Civil War Hero."

Five months later, Lee returned to his true love: education. Turning down offers of charity, he took the presidency of Washington College, a small, bankrupt college in Lexington, Va. He thought education would help the South recover from the war, Kavanagh and Murdoch note.

In his new job, Lee inspired young students, not soldiers.

Lee memorized students' names and asked about their lives. He urged professors to give special care to struggling students, notes Margaret Sanborn in "Robert E. Lee: A Portrait." Lee's dictum: "Always observe the stage driver's rules. Take care of the poor horses."

In honor of his leadership, the school today is called Washington and Lee University.

Lee showed by example the advice he gave his children: "Live in the world you inhabit. Look upon things as they are. Take them as you find them. Make the best of them. Turn them to your advantage."

14

Gen. Colin Powell

Climbed To The Top By Always Doing His Best

Summer jobs were scarce for teen-agers growing up in the Bronx in the early 1950s. Businesses didn't often need teens. But young Colin Powell needed money. And he was determined to find a way to make it.

So he showed up early every morning at the Teamsters Hall to volunteer for day jobs. Every once in a while, he'd get lucky and snare a spot as a helper on a soda delivery truck.

Then a position opened as a porter at a Pepsi plant. None of the white kids volunteered. Powell, however, eagerly accepted the messy job. A job was a job, he figured. He spent the summer carefully cleaning up sticky soda syrup. He did such a good job the plant foreman invited him back the following summer. And when he returned, he operated a bottling machine, not a mop. By the end of that second summer, he was a deputy shift leader. It was an experience that taught him a valuable lesson.

"All work is honorable," he said in his memoir, "My American Journey." "Always do your best, because someone is watching."

Powell looked for a way to do just that and learn something at the same time. He did his research and discovered he could join ROTC and learn about the Army. Fascinated by the military, Powell jumped at the chance.

Worked Hard

Powell found his calling in ROTC.

"I not only liked it, but I was pretty good at it," he said in a 1998 address to the Academy of Achievement. "That's really what you have to look for in life — something that you like and something that you think you're pretty good at."

At the City College of New York, he continued his policy of always doing his best. He excelled in his ROTC courses, was offered a regular Army commission and, over the next 30 years, worked his way up to chairman of the Joint Chiefs of Staff, the highest-ranking military position in the U.S. armed forces.

Among the honors of his highly decorated career, Powell earned two Purple Hearts, the Bronze Star, a Soldier's Medal and the Legion of Merit for his two tours of duty in Vietnam.

Early on in ROTC, Powell began showing strengths that he'd use throughout his career. He started to look for creative solutions. He'd look at a situation and break it down, examining each piece of information. This allowed him to see problems and find answers where others couldn't.

For example, as the pledge officer of the Pershing Rifles, the ROTC fraternity, Powell had to decide how to attract new members. He could've done what all the other fraternities on campus did — show dirty movies. But he opted to come up with a more original alternative.

"Let's show movies of what we do, like drill competitions," he said. "Let's show them what we're all about."

That semester, the Pershing Rifles attracted the largest pledge class in years. "This was a defining moment for me," he said. "The first small indication I might be able to influence events."

Powell also recognized his mistakes and learned from them. Elected company commander of the Pershing Rifles, he knew a close friend was distracted from his job as head of the fraternity's trick drill team.

But instead of stepping in and demanding that his friend focus on the drill team, Powell let him slide. He didn't relieve his friend, and the team didn't win its competition.

"I was angry with myself," Powell said. "I had failed the trick drill team. . . . I learned being in charge means making decisions, no matter how unpleasant. If it's broke, fix it. You cannot let the mission suffer or make the majority pay to spare the feelings of an individual."

Powell tried to figure out what was most important to him, and then focus on that. He didn't allow side issues to knock him off track. Even when that side issue was racism.

Powell first experienced racism when assigned to Fort Benning in Georgia. Before, he'd been recognized for his achievements, not his skin color. In Georgia, he suffered slurs and was ignored in restaurants. When first confronted with racism, he didn't know how — or even if — he could cope.

But he refused to let the anger he felt at others' ignorance distract him from his goals. "I began by identifying my priorities," he said. "I wanted above all to succeed in my Army career. I didn't intend to give way to a self-destructive rage no matter how provoked."

It paid off. He kept working hard and treating everyone with courtesy. His superiors saw his efforts and rewarded him, steadily promoting him through the ranks.

Powell realized early on that there were lessons to be learned everywhere. For example, after graduating from the Army's Ranger school, he was assigned to an infantry company in Germany. His company commanding officer was the Army equivalent of permanent middle management, a guy barely hanging on and more likely to be pushed out of service than promoted.

Still, Powell said, "There was something appealing about him, something to be learned, something not taught on the plains at West Point or in texts on military science and tactics."

Early in his tour of duty there, Powell lost his sidearm. The loss of his weapon could've ruined his career before it started. But that same CO found the weapon and gave it back to Powell without reporting it to higher authorities.

This "example of humane leadership that does not always go by the book was not lost on me. When (members of your team) fall, pick 'em up, dust 'em off, pat 'em on the back and move 'em on."

Knew His Strengths

Powell feels it's important to know your strengths. "But it's also important to know your weaknesses," he said. "That way, a good leader can surround himself with people who complement his skills."

"In every successful military organization — and I suspect in all successful enterprises — different styles of leadership have to be present," he said. "If a top man has vision and vision only, he requires a whip hand to enforce his ideas. If an organization has a visionary and a whip, it needs a chaplain to soften the relentless demands of the others."

This understanding of leadership structure has apparently guided Powell in his role as secretary of state since 2001 under President George W. Bush.

"It's also important to be able to turn a negative into a positive," Powell says. Take the time he was in the 2nd Brigade of the 101st Airborne and two other brigades were picked to join a valuable training exercise in Europe.

Powell didn't sulk because he was left behind. Instead, he decided to make the best of a bad situation. While the others were overseas, he got every officer in his brigade — including the chaplains — air assault qualified, a considerable achievement in the short period the others were away.

"If you get the dirty end of the stick," he said, "sharpen it and turn it into a useful tool."

15

American Indian Leader Tecumseh

His Honesty And Character Brought Tribes Together

Tecumseh was just a minor Shawnee chief in what is now the Ohio-Indiana region. Yet he forged the farthest-reaching bonds ever among Indians in North America.

How did Tecumseh (1768–1813) do it? By standing for integrity, even among foes. He even risked looking like a softy to his peers.

Torturing enemies was a common way Indians marked their wins. But Tecumseh spoke out against the practice when he was just 16 years old, reports Allan Eckert in "A Sorrow in Our Heart: The Life of Tecumseh."

It paid off. Fellow Indians revered Tecumseh for taking the high ground. And they trusted him more as a result.

Tecumseh was the only one of the Indian leaders to grasp that the European settlers viewed land completely differently than did Indians. It gave him a broader vision that enabled him to communicate equally well with his Indian brethren and the whites, making him one of the greatest American Indian leaders of all time.

Tecumseh also earned respect by making sure all of his people were able to escape advancing enemy armies during battles. He wouldn't retreat until he was sure everyone was safe.

He taught his tribe to have high standards. He urged Indians to change their way of life by curbing alcohol intake and turning to ethics and spirituality.

"He was noted for his frankness and put a high premium on truth," said John Sugden in "Tecumseh: A Life."

How did Tecumseh learn the value of honesty? By practice. When he told the truth, people learned to trust him.

"The implicit obedience and respect which the followers of Tecumseh pay to him is really astonishing, and more than any other circumstance bespeaks him one of those uncommon geniuses which spring up occasionally to produce revolutions and overturn the established order of things," wrote William Henry Harrison, who won the American presidency for directing the forces that killed Tecumseh in the Battle of the Thames near Thamesville, Ontario.

Growing Up Quickly

Tecumseh was forced to take responsibility early in life. His father was killed by Americans when he was 6 years old — so it was up to him to begin hunting to provide for his family at that age.

With daily practice, he became so skillful that he could bring in three times as many deer or buffalo as anyone else in a day. He was made a warrior at age 12, several years earlier than usual.

Tecumseh was also known for having a positive attitude. He always credited others who played key roles in his successes in hunting and war.

He set lofty goals and focused on them. Tecumseh gave his life to uniting Indians from the Great Lakes to the Gulf of Mexico. That was the only way to stop the American attacks on native lands, he said.

To make that happen, Tecumseh faced a great task. He had to get those who saw themselves only as members of tribes to feel part of a larger group of Indians. Intertribal conflict, language differences, cultural gaps and geography created barriers for Tecumseh.

"The eternal optimist brought astounding energy" to the challenge, though, Sugden wrote, and taught Indians to see themselves as one. Tecumseh's persistence helped him gain a following as far away as Florida.

How'd he win over the tribes? Through his ability to communicate.

Tecumseh learned the importance of speaking well by sitting around campfires when he was a child. He saw how the best story-tellers captured the attention of the entire tribe. He listened to the top speakers each night and kept mental notes of what worked and what didn't.

The next thing Tecumseh did to be a good speaker was to travel widely with two of his brothers. Meeting Indians from various tribes allowed him to get to know them and their languages.

He took any chance he could to practice speaking. He often stood up in front of a tribe he was visiting and started talking. That helped him to become one of the most fluent speakers that anyone — both whites and Indians — had ever heard.

Creativity was another of Tecumseh's best weapons. He'd find ways to pierce enemy lines that no one expected.

At age 23, he disguised himself and entered American forts a number of times to listen to soldiers talk. The intelligence helped Tecumseh lead the greatest defeat inflicted by Indians on the U.S. Army. At the Battle of Wabash River, 832 American soldiers were killed, in comparison with 264 at Little Bighorn.

A Triumph In War

Tecumseh's innovation also helped his small army, along with 830 British troops, to force 2,500 American soldiers at Fort Detroit to surrender during the War of 1812.

How? He had his 530 men walk through a clearing that could be seen from the fort. But Tecumseh had them walk in a circle so each warrior appeared many times. The Americans panicked, believing they were being attacked by thousands of Indians.

The capture of the fort ended the American drive into Canada. But it wasn't enough to secure Tecumseh's dream.

Shortly thereafter, Adm. Oliver Perry defeated the British fleet on Lake Erie against all odds. That marked the beginning of the end of the war. As British fortunes waned, so did Tecumseh's dream of a native union.

Yet the strength of Tecumseh's character made him the most revered of all American Indian leaders.

"A great body of mythology has grown around him, often clouding the wonderfully impressive facts of his life. There is no need for that, since his character and accomplishments alone establish him as one of the finer human beings in recorded history," Eckert wrote.

16

Soldier-Statesman
George Marshall
Winning The War And Peace

George Catlett Marshall was the highest-ranking cadet officer in his class when he graduated from the Virginia Military Institute in 1901.

And he was dead set on becoming one of the 1,200 new second lieutenants the U.S. Army was about to commission.

He had the grades, and he had the experience. He also had political connections — he came from a wealthy Virginia family that descended from John Marshall, the nation's third chief justice.

But Marshall (1880–1959) was too determined to rely on anyone else to get what he wanted.

Instead, he decided that to make sure he landed the commission, he had to go straight to the top — and pay a visit to the White House.

He was assured he'd never get in to see President William McKinley, but Marshall persisted. He waited around for hours, then intrepidly attached himself to the tail end of a group going into the president's office.

When the others left, "Mr. McKinley in a very nice manner asked what I wanted, and I stated my case," Marshall later recalled.

Moving Up

That bold stroke got him his commission, setting in motion one of the nation's most important military careers. Praised by Winston Churchill as the "organizer of victory" in World War II, Marshall engineered the buildup of the U.S. military from 175,000 men in 1939 to 8 million strong, and he devised the grand strategy for bringing that force to bear.

Marshall's contribution to the peace was as critical as his wartime service. As secretary of state in 1947, he proposed and fought for what quickly became known as the Marshall Plan to rehabilitate the devastated economies of Europe with billions in American aid and create a bulwark against communism. In 1953, in honor of this contribution, Marshall became the only career soldier ever to receive the Nobel Peace Prize.

Marshall always stood up for what he believed in, even at the risk of hurting his career.

As a 36-year-old captain, Marshall was with the first U.S. contingent to arrive in France in 1917 and helped direct military exercises to ready untrained soldiers for combat.

The lack of combat-ready forces put Gen. John Pershing, the commander of the American Expeditionary Force, under extreme pressure from the Allies. Impatient for reinforcements, Pershing vented his frustration and humiliated Marshall's superior officers with a tirade that Marshall felt was unjust.

"Marshall — literally taking his own career in his hands — reached out and tapped the turning Pershing on the arm," wrote Alan Saunders in "A General for Peace."

"General Pershing, there is something to be said here and I think I should say it," Marshall said, launching into an angry rebuttal.

Witnesses, including the officers he defended, were certain Marshall's military career was over. But the outburst won Pershing's respect, and the general often sought Marshall's advice.

"By the summer of 1918, Marshall would be a temporary colonel on Pershing's own staff and within two years his personal aide," wrote Mark Stoler in "Soldier-Statesman of the American Century."

Straight Shooter

In late 1938, when Marshall was among a handful of generals that Franklin Roosevelt was considering for the Army's chief of staff, the president detailed his plans at a White House meeting to seek a military funding increase from Congress.

While others at the meeting strongly disagreed with the president's request, which was strictly focused on building up air power, only Marshall voiced his disapproval.

Instead of derailing his chances, Marshall's willingness to speak his mind impressed the president, and Marshall was sworn in as chief of staff on Sept. 1, 1939, the same day Germany invaded Poland.

Marshall expected the same frankness from his subordinates.

He made this demand in the clearest terms to Dean Acheson, who served under Marshall at the State Department and later became secretary of state. "I shall expect the most complete frankness, particularly about myself. I have no feelings except those I reserve for Mrs. Marshall," he told Acheson.

Marshall surrounded himself with the best people he could find, and he didn't hesitate to remove those he deemed ineffective.

Throughout his career, Marshall relentlessly pruned deadwood. This trait was first evident at Fort Benning, Ga., where Marshall served as head of the academic department beginning in 1927.

"He was ruthless with his faculty," Saunders wrote. "Those that did not come up to par were quickly weeded out."

The results spoke for themselves, as Marshall turned out an impressive crop of officers, including Omar Bradley, George Patton, Joseph Stilwell and Maxwell Taylor.

When Marshall set about readying the U.S. military for war in 1939, he was even more exacting.

"Only one of the 1939 senior generals would survive his purge and command troops in battle during World War II," Stoler wrote.

In their place, Marshall installed people listed in his "little black book," which he'd been filling with names of officers who impressed him since his days at Fort Benning.

As war approached, the challenges Marshall faced were monumental, from building up the greatest war machine in history to getting funds from Congress for the U.S. and her allies, while dealing with crises breaking out all over the world.

Integrity was Marshall's greatest asset. Without it, he wouldn't have won the support he needed in Congress during the war and in gaining approval of the Marshall Plan.

"He would tell the truth even if it hurt his cause," House Speaker Sam Rayburn recalled after the war. "Congress always respected him and would give him things they would give no one else."

In accepting the post of secretary of state, Marshall made it clear he would never run for office. That dispelled any concern from Congress that cooperating with Marshall might elevate a future political rival.

The Right Name

President Harry S. Truman called the $17 billion European Recovery Program the Marshall Plan to depoliticize the legislation and help it pass a Republican-led Congress.

"Can you imagine its chances of passage in an election year in a Republican Congress if it is named for Truman and not Marshall?" the president asked an aide.

Just days after retiring as Army chief of staff in November 1945, Marshall returned home only to receive a call from Truman asking him to go to China as a special envoy. Marshall didn't think of declining then, or when Truman later asked him to serve as secretary of state and secretary of defense.

17

John Pershing
Dedicated General Led Charge
From The Philippines
To Europe

As a young captain assigned to duty in the Philippines in 1901, John Pershing had his work cut out for him.

The U.S. had won claim to the Philippines by defeating Spain. But the Moros, the fierce warriors of the interior, refused to submit to American rule. That wasn't a surprise. They hadn't accepted Spain's rule for two centuries.

Pershing (1860–1948) knew that information was his best weapon. So when he first arrived on Mindanao, the second largest island in the archipelago, he steeped himself in the language, culture and history of the local residents.

Aware that friendliness builds better relationships than force, Pershing ordered his troops to be cordial and pleasant toward the Moros when they came into town to trade on Saturdays. He introduced himself and talked to them. A prominent local chief, called a *datto*, visited him. Pershing returned the visit, walking into the jungle unarmed.

His methods worked. Eventually, the dattos accepted him as one of their own.

Pershing's commanding general asked him to encircle Lake Lanao, a 138-square-mile body of water high in the mountains, as a show of American strength. With 500 men and 400 pack animals, he accomplished the difficult feat. It was widely covered in the U.S. press and made Pershing a household name.

"He was acclaimed as the soldier-diplomat, showing the flag in velvet-glove-over-fist-of-steel, his gleaming battle-ax raised but not wantonly employed, a conqueror with better motives and finer accomplishments than, say, Cortez," wrote biographer Gene Smith in "Until the Last Trumpet Sounds: The Life of General of the Army's John J. Pershing."

Chasing Pancho Villa

Pershing became the best-known American military leader of his time. He was a part of every major campaign through World War I. President Theodore Roosevelt praised Pershing's courage under fire while commanding a company invading Cuba during the Spanish-American War.

Pershing chased Pancho Villa back into Mexico after the bandit terrorized American travelers and shot up the town of Columbia, N.M. Pershing never captured him, but he achieved his mission, which was to disperse his gang.

Pershing's crowning achievement was as commanding officer of 3 million American men in Europe during World War I. He had to train soldiers in a hurry.

But he trained them well. So confident in their training was Pershing that he demanded that American troops fight as a unit, rather than pair up with their French or British allies. The Yanks held against terrifying German attacks, and Pershing returned home a national hero.

Pershing saw every problem as a challenge. As a brigadier general on a second tour in the Philippines in 1913, he was head of U.S. forces in the Philippines attempting to disarm the Moros. Some agreed to turn in their arms, but others refused and took refuge on the extinct volcano Bud Bagsak.

Pershing didn't want to attack because women and children were with the rebels. So he tried another approach. He ordered his troops out of the area, and soon many Moros and their families returned to their homes. Pershing considered the men who remained on the mountain hard-core criminals.

He quickly and quietly assembled a 1,200-man force and attacked. The Moros counterattacked with fury. Then the American line started to break against the Moro assault.

Leading by example, Pershing personally moved into the breach, encouraging his men to hold. They did. Not a single Moro surrendered. They died to the last man.

Civil War Baby

Pershing was born just as the Civil War was beginning. His father ran the general store and post office in Laclede, Mo., where families were divided over which side to join.

From his father, Pershing learned to stand up for what he believed in. The older Pershing, for example, flew the Stars and Stripes over his house despite threats to remove it. He also sold supplies to Union soldiers, who to young Pershing were bigger-than-life heroes.

After the war, the store prospered. Pershing's father bought land and became one of the area's richest men. But he was overextended and lost everything in the Panic of 1873. He turned to farming and faced a plague of locusts, then drought.

Young Pershing's dreams of attending law school had to be shelved. But not permanently. Pershing was determined he'd get there one day. To support himself in the meantime, he taught at a school for black children while studying law on his own.

He was attending a summer session at a teaching school when he saw an advertisement for the examination to enter West Point. Intrigued, he applied and took the test. He won the appointment and was off on a military career.

Despite his drive, Pershing was just an above-average student. He received demerits, usually for tardiness, while many cadets got through West Point with none. He struggled with French — although he learned enough French history to be credited with his most famous line upon leading the Americans into Paris in 1917: "Lafayette, we are here!"

Pershing excelled under West Point's discipline. It inspired him to strive to improve himself.

"At West Point a perhaps inborn distaste for haziness, sloppiness, imprecision, haphazardness was summed up in the phrase that

epitomized him then and afterward: 'Let's get where we're going,'"
wrote Smith.

Stoic and determined, Pershing believed that when you make a
commitment, it should be honored. Even at great personal cost.

During an assignment in San Francisco in 1915, Pershing's wife
and three of his four children were killed in a blaze at his home. Pershing's superiors sympathetically told him he could take some time
off. Though devastated, Pershing refused. He vowed to uphold his
commitment to his country. Just a year later, he led the expedition
against Pancho Villa.

Tough But Fair

Pershing strove to act with integrity. Once, a group of American
Indians bet him he couldn't win a foot race. He won. But he refused
to collect on the bet, and forbade his men from collecting on bets
they made with the Indians.

Both as a teacher and a soldier, Pershing was demanding but fair.
As a training officer at the University of Nebraska, he taught military courses. The courses were required, but taken lightly.

He changed that. He insisted that students push for perfection
in their close-order drills. He inspired a joy and pride in the students
as he taught them. Soon, students were practicing on their own.

He led a drill team called the Pershing Rifles in a national competition in Omaha. The team won with many students and the university president on hand. It was as big a win as any the Cornhuskers
have had since.

And, at Nebraska, he achieved his childhood goal of getting a
law degree.

PART 3

True Leaders Fight For What They Believe In

It is impossible to write about great causes without living for those great causes, to be a great poet without being a great human being. Man must discover again, within himself, a deeper sense of responsibility toward the world, which means responsibility toward something higher than self.

— Vaclav Havel

18

President Abraham Lincoln

His Focus Helped Him Preserve The Union

Abraham Lincoln was desperate. He'd fired, one after another, four generals who'd led the Union forces. It was 1863, and the Civil War had dragged on far too long.

Over and over, Lincoln had appointed commanders who were well dressed, well spoken and well educated. Trouble was, they wilted in battle. They made bad decisions. They retreated at crucial moments. They lacked results.

If there was one thing Lincoln couldn't stand, it was bad leadership. In the end, his drive for excellent leadership brought the Civil War to an end and made Lincoln one of America's greatest presidents.

Lincoln (1809–65) held the office of president from 1861 until his death. He was inaugurated on March 4, 1861, and the Civil War began on April 12 of the same year.

"It was Lincoln who led the nation through its greatest crisis and preserved the United States," wrote Russell Shorto in "Abraham Lincoln: To Preserve the Union."

"He was a man to match the mountains and the sea," wrote Edwin Markham in his poem, "Lincoln, the Man of the People."

Picking The Right Personnel

Lincoln knew he couldn't be the only leader, though. To win the war, he'd have to find other leaders to help him in his charge.

In 1863, Lincoln heard about fiery Gen. Ulysses S. Grant, who'd just led a successful and brilliant assault on Vicksburg, Miss. Yet Lincoln's aides told him not to bother considering Grant for the position of commanding general. Why? Grant was rude, they said. He dressed in rumpled clothes. He didn't speak properly.

But only one thing mattered to Lincoln at that point: Could Grant do the job? Could he successfully defeat Confederate Gen. Robert E. Lee?

Presidential aides agreed that Grant was a masterful leader on the battlefield. His drive toward victory was single-minded, passionate and inspiring.

From talking to others and conducting his own research, Lincoln knew Grant was the right man — regardless of how he talked or dressed. He offered Grant the job and the title of general in chief. In the end, Grant's drive and strategy in battle brought the Confederacy to its knees.

It wasn't the first time Lincoln acted on his beliefs against the wishes of others. Despite the feelings of some Northerners, Lincoln avowedly fought against slavery. In 1863, he issued the Emancipation Proclamation, freeing all slaves in Confederate-held territory.

Throughout the war, Lincoln stayed fixed on one goal — preserving the unity of the U.S. "A house divided against itself cannot stand," he said.

"He encouraged debate among his advisers. Lincoln liked the honesty," Shorto wrote. "The spirited men whom Lincoln had chosen for his Cabinet often argued loudly with one another and with the president over his conduct of war."

But when it came to the question of national unity, Lincoln was firm. Since boyhood, Lincoln had made national unity one of his top values. Growing up in what is now Spencer County, Ind., he read everything he could get his hands on. One book that influenced him heavily was "The Life of George Washington," by Mason Locke Weems.

Young Lincoln read the book until he could quote whole paragraphs. He was inspired as he read about Washington's battles for liberty. "I recollect thinking then, boy even though I was, that there must have been something more than common that these men struggled for," Lincoln said.

He continued, "This Union, the Constitution, and the liberties of the people, shall be perpetuated in accordance with the original idea for which that struggle was made."

The Bible also moved Lincoln. He read it over and over, and he would copy entire passages of Scripture on rough paper with a charcoal pencil so he could memorize them.

Let Justice Prevail

He believed in justice wholeheartedly, even for the smallest creatures. As a youngster, he often gave speeches against cruelty to animals. "An ant's life is as sweet to it as ours is to us," he said in a speech at age 15, after he'd seen a group of boys torturing a turtle.

By the time he was 17, Lincoln decided he wanted to practice law so he could make sure justice prevailed. He read several books on the subject, but he knew that wouldn't be enough. He needed to see good lawyers in action. So Lincoln regularly walked 17 miles to the county courthouse to get a firsthand glimpse of the proceedings there.

"He sat in the back of the courtroom for hours and watched the way the lawyers shook their fists as they argued their cases. He watched their faces go red as they got more and more excited. He listened to their carefully constructed arguments. When he got back home, he had a month of thinking to do about all he had heard," Shorto wrote.

In 1830, the Lincoln family moved to a farm outside Decatur, Ill. Lincoln worked a number of odd jobs. But he never forgot about his dream to practice law. With each job, he challenged himself to learn at least one skill that'd help him in the legal profession.

When he worked as a shopkeeper, he focused on being honest and fair with all his transactions. Once, for example, when he accidentally shortchanged a woman by 6 cents, he followed her home so that he could give her the difference.

When he worked as a postmaster, he sharpened his people skills. As a land surveyor, he pushed himself to be precise. In 1834, he ran for and was elected to the Illinois Legislature, where he got his first taste of politics. Because it didn't pay much, he kept moonlighting as a surveyor.

He was often heard to say, not in jest, but seriously, as if he were deeply impressed, rather than elated, with the idea: "I shall some day be president of the United States," wrote Francis Fisher Browne, one of Lincoln's early biographers, in "The Every-Day Life of Abraham Lincoln."

At night, he'd hit the law books. "He pursued (his) study at odd hours, stolen from sleep," Browne wrote. In 1836, he passed the bar and began practicing law with a Springfield, Ill., firm.

In politics, Lincoln met with some success, but he suffered failure as well. He was elected to the U.S. House of Representatives in 1846, but he did not seek re-election in 1848. He ran for the U.S. Senate in 1858 and lost to Stephen A. Douglas after a famous series of debates.

With each failure, though, Lincoln pushed himself to become more informed, acute and decisive. He was patient, and he kept faith that he was headed to the top.

In 1860, Lincoln became the second presidential candidate of the young Republican Party and was elected. On Dec. 20, 1860, South Carolina seceded from the Union. By April 1861, the country was embroiled in the Civil War.

Members of his own Cabinet doubted Lincoln could handle the war. Each believed that Lincoln, the backwoods lawyer, was "too raw and untried to deal with the overwhelming crisis at hand," Shorto wrote.

What Lincoln lacked in experience he made up for in hard work. Often, he'd be at his desk before 6 a.m., studying war reports. He'd stay there until after midnight. He took the war one battle at a time, one decision at a time and one tactical move at a time.

What kept him motivated? A dream of a unified country — and disgust for a job left undone. "With malice toward none, with charity for all, with firmness in the right as God gives us to see the right, let us strive on to finish the work we are in," he said in his Second Inaugural Address on March 4, 1865.

Lee surrendered to Grant on April 9, 1865. Six days later, Lincoln died after being shot at a theater performance in Washington, D.C.

19

Aviator Billy Mitchell
His Efforts Helped Build A Separate Air Force

Nothing stopped Airman Billy Mitchell. Not even a court-martial. Mitchell was a World War I airman and career Army officer who dedicated his life to the creation of the Air Force.

In fact, he was so convinced that a new air branch of the military was needed to defend the U.S. that he sacrificed his Army career to the cause. Mitchell waged a loud campaign that embarrassed the military's hidebound brass, wielding the press and public opinion as his weapons.

When the Army court-martialed him in 1925 on charges of insubordination and conduct prejudicial to the service, he was found guilty, after which he quit the Army and kept on fighting.

That was no small thing. Prior to his campaign, he'd risen to the rank of brigadier general.

Big Picture

Mitchell (1879–1936), the son of a wealthy Wisconsin banker who became a U.S. senator, first grew convinced of the key role planes would play in military conflict long before the "Great War," as World War I was first called.

As author Burke Davis recounted in "The Billy Mitchell Affair," Mitchell wrote as early as 1906 that "conflicts no doubt will be carried on in the future in the air."

Ten years later, when he was in his mid-30s and the Army began sending up planes, Mitchell asked his superiors for flight training. They told him he was too old.

Undeterred, Mitchell paid for lessons out of his own pocket.

An incident in his childhood illustrates who shaped his drive. As a youngster, he fell off a pony and told his mother that he couldn't ride.

Her response: "You go on riding it until you can." By the time he was 14, he was playing polo.

The man the Army passed over for flight training understood air power's potential better than anyone else in uniform.

In fact, a higher-ranking general made way for Mitchell to lead U.S. squadrons in France. Mitchell led the American Expeditionary Force's aviation support for ground troops in World War I.

His tour was so successful that he was decorated not only by the U.S., but by several European countries as well.

Returning to the U.S. as a celebrity, he began to wage his own war for a separate air service.

He was no stranger to political battle. When Billy was a teen, he lived on Capitol Hill with his father, Sen. John Mitchell. In fact, he wanted to live in Washington so much that he begged to get out of a Racine, Wis. prep school.

Mitchell was the first soldier to attack the military publicly for its passive stance on air power. He knew how to curry friends among the press. His Prohibition-era parties flowed with liquor.

But Mitchell didn't just hold soirees.

He showed the press and the country the power of surprise air attacks on U.S. soil.

In 1921, he spotlighted the Navy's looming inferiority as the nation's first line of defense. In bombing tests in 1921, Mitchell's crews sank the captured German battleship Ostfriesland from the air, exceeding expectations of the military brass.

And that was the first of many ship sinkings.

Solid Perseverance

His standing with the press and public soared, but the military wouldn't budge.

So Mitchell simulated mock bombing runs over New York City and other Eastern cities. The press ran accounts of them, too.

"He was always good for a story and good for a pose," said Walter Boyne, author of "Beyond the Wild Blue: A History of the United States Air Force, 1947–1997." "He had a good sense of public relations, and he had people working for him who understood it."

Mitchell's superiors shipped him to Hawaii to keep him out of the papers. It was a bad move.

Follow-up tours of Europe and Asia led Mitchell to pen a 323-page report in 1924 warning of growing Japanese air power.

He predicted that Japan would one day direct an air attack against Pearl Harbor and Clark Field in the Philippines. The report went largely ignored, but Mitchell pressed forward.

In 1925, when a naval seaplane was lost and a Navy dirigible crashed, Mitchell told reporters they were the result of "criminal negligence, and the almost treasonable negligence of our national defense by the War and Navy departments."

His oral statement was backed by a 6,000-word indictment of the armed forces' campaign to prevent the development of a separate air service.

His fate was sealed as he faced a court-martial. But Mitchell didn't suffer silently.

Following a guilty verdict, he resigned and quickly embarked on a four-month lecture tour, warning of the dangers of a lack of military preparedness.

For the next decade, citizen Mitchell kept right on pushing his campaign through dozens of newspaper and magazine articles and two books.

Over and over, he warned that future wars would be decided by aerial bombings of vital industrial installations.

He proposed a special corps of mechanics, troop-carrying aircraft and long-range bombers. He encouraged Army pilots to set records for speed, endurance and altitude to keep aviation in the news.

"Had he not done what he had done, and sown the seeds, we wouldn't have seen an independent air force in 1947," Boyne said.

A decade after his premature death at the age of 56, Congress voted Mitchell a posthumous medal for his "foresight in the field of military aviation."

20

Gen. Benjamin Davis
Proved His Heroism In Face Of War And Racial Prejudice

Benjamin O. Davis Jr. knew that actions were much louder than words. And he needed something loud.

Davis (1912–2002) was rejected by the Army Air Corps in 1935. He was physically and academically qualified due to his standing at West Point, but the Army wouldn't train blacks to be pilots.

Davis refused to forget his dream of becoming an Army pilot. Over five years he repeatedly applied for pilot training, only to be shut out. When the Roosevelt administration ordered the War Department to create a black flying unit in 1940, his dream finally became a reality.

The unit became known as the "Tuskegee Airmen," and it eventually grew to 992 pilots. Davis, the first black airman to earn his wings, won command of the 99th Pursuit Squadron. He rose to become the Air Force's first black brigadier general in 1965.

"My own opinion was that blacks could best overcome racist attitudes through their achievements, even though those achievements had to take place within the hateful environment of segregation," Davis wrote in his autobiography, "Benjamin O. Davis, Jr.: American."

High Stakes

While being trained at Tuskegee Army Air Field in Alabama, Davis knew that to make a real difference, he and his men had to do more than earn their wings.

"I (was) aware of the high-stakes game we were about to be involved in. Even at that early date it was apparent to us that the lot of blacks in the postwar military and particularly in the postwar Air Corps would be largely determined by black combat performance during the war," he said.

With the onset of World War II, Davis was promoted to lieutenant colonel in March 1942. The 99th Pursuit Squadron was deployed to North Africa in May 1943.

Davis, a disciplinarian, didn't accept excuses. He expected his men to adhere to Army regulations. He was scrupulously honest, highly disciplined and a stickler for detail.

"I had a great affection for (the men), although as their commander I consciously tempered the warmth I felt for each of them with an insistence on high standards of performance," Davis said.

He flew 60 combat missions in total, first with the 99th, and then with the all-black 332nd Fighter Group, which was deployed to Italy in January 1944.

Under Davis and later, the 99th distinguished itself in combat. Davis' 332nd flew more than 15,000 sorties against the German Luftwaffe. His outfit shot down 111 enemy planes and destroyed another 150 on the ground. The 332nd lost just 66 of its own planes.

Davis kept himself and his men focused on their mission. In December 1943, Gen. Ira Eaker, commander of the 15th Air Force, told Davis of his displeasure with the escort protection some white fighter groups were providing heavy bombers, such as B-24s.

Eaker thought many of these white pilots were seeking enemy planes to shoot down for their own glory at the expense of their mission. On some missions, as many as 25 heavy bombers, with crews of 11 men each, were lost.

Eaker wanted commanders to ensure the protection of those planes. Davis promised his orders would be carried out. Under Davis, the 332nd completed about 200 escort missions without losing one heavy bomber.

"That was one thing (Davis) was on us night and day about. Doing the job, the way it was planned," said Lt. Col. John Suggs in "Black Knights: The Story of the Tuskegee Airmen," by Lynn Homan and Thomas Reilly.

On June 9, 1944, three days after D-Day, Davis and 39 of his P-47 fighters escorted a group of B-24s to Munich, Germany, on a bombing mission. More than 100 German fighters attacked them, but the 332nd fought them off. Davis received the Distinguished Flying Cross for leadership and bravery.

He eventually received the Silver Star for gallantry in action, and other honors. But he never forgot he was part of a team effort.

"As gratified as I was to receive this personal recognition, I understood that it was truly a recognition for the men of the 332nd Fighter Group, and that my success as their commander had depended entirely on their support and conscientious efforts," he said.

Groundbreaking Efforts

Davis' performance in command and that of his men, who themselves earned several medals, opened the door for integration of the Armed Forces in 1948.

"In addition to physical courage, Davis had moral courage. When the Air Force was pushing segregation, Davis stood for integration. Career men don't do that. They do whatever the leadership wants," said Alan Gropman, chairman of the department of grand strategy and mobilization at the Industrial College of the Armed Forces.

"Gen. Davis' leadership convinced military commanders that segregation was unnecessary and therefore an unconscionable waste," he said.

Davis' role model was his father, Gen. Benjamin O. Davis Sr. The senior Davis was barred from West Point because of his color, but he persevered as an enlisted man and became America's first black general.

"Throughout my own military career and beyond, his achievements stood as an example of what could be accomplished in the face of seemingly impossible social opposition," he said.

Davis was a living embodiment of the West Point motto of "Duty, Honor, Country," but his academy experience was unhappy. The white cadets talked with him only in the line of duty. They hoped to make him so unhappy he'd resign. They failed.

"What they did not realize was that I was stubborn enough to put up with their treatment to reach the goal I had come to attain,"

Davis said. He was the first black cadet to graduate from West Point in the 20th century.

Davis held a variety of increasingly responsible posts in the integrated Air Force, and he retired as deputy commander in chief of the U.S. Strike Command. He retired from government in 1975 and lived for many years in Arlington, Va.

21

Ahmed Shah Massoud

The Lion of Panjshir
Roared Against Oppression

Ahmed Shah Massoud's goal was freedom. It cost him his life. Massoud, the first hero of Sept. 11, died two days earlier. Two al-Qaida suicide bombers posing as Belgian journalists killed him with an exploding camera at his camp in Afghanistan's remote Panjshir Valley.

Massoud fought for democracy in Afghanistan for 23 years. He battled the Soviet army and Taliban with few troops and meager supplies.

Afghans began to call him the "Lion of Panjshir" after he repulsed nine Soviet attacks in the 1980s. He kept the Taliban and al-Qaida at bay for five years.

He died unable to fathom U.S. abandonment of his anti-Soviet, anti-Taliban fighters. Nor could he comprehend U.S. backing for Pakistan, whose infamous intelligence service had created the Taliban.

Americans don't realize what they owe Massoud, says historian Sebastian Junger, author of "The Perfect Storm" and "Fire."

Massoud made America's victory in Afghanistan possible, says Junger, who spent a month with Massoud for *National Geographic Adventure* magazine in 2000. "Had he not held out against the Taliban for so many years, militarily what we would have faced would have been vastly more complicated and costly," he said.

A friend of Massoud agrees. "If al-Qaida had taken the Panjshir Valley, there would be no way to get them out," said photographer

Reza Deghati, who uses only his first name professionally. The Iranian national lives in exile in Paris.

Said Junger: "We ignored Massoud's warnings about what was happening there. The connection between his assassination and 9-11 is absolute. I had interviewed a Taliban prisoner. He said, 'We have to kill Massoud. He's the last wall standing between us and our goal.'"

"That goal was a militant Islamist belt from Sinkiang to Chechnya," said Haron Amin, deputy chief of the Afghan mission in Washington, D.C.

Man Of Vision

Massoud had a vision for his country, says Amin, Massoud's emissary in the U.S. It was one of social justice, tranquility and progress, keeping the Islamic character but integrating women into politics and the labor force.

His intellect, leadership, humanitarianism and war record made him a figure of mythic proportions. His death was such a blow to Massoud's Northern Alliance that his aides kept it a secret for four days.

"We wept at night and lied in the day," said Amin. "We had become orphans."

Massoud valued education above all else, says Amin. That meant for women, too.

He wanted to be an engineer. He went to the French-language high school in Kabul and studied engineering at Kabul's polytechnic college.

He left the college to fight the Moscow-backed communist government. He became a guerrilla in 1979 when the Soviets invaded to prop up their puppet regime.

Though Massoud gave up his education to fight, his engineering skills made him a great field commander, says Junger. He could build anything. He had an incredible talent for strategy and tactics.

He always found time for his first love, education, says Junger. Once on the way back from the front, he stopped to inspect a rebuilt school. The children's desks were made from ammo crates. Massoud said they were too small. He asked the carpenters to make them bigger.

That episode reflected Massoud's personal dream. "During the Soviet war, I asked Massoud, 'What is the best job for yourself when

the Soviets are gone?' He said, 'Teacher in a Panjshir village,'"
recalled Reza.

Behind the dream was an iron will, says Reza. "I saw this in 1985.
The Soviet army surrounded 90% of the Panjshir. Massoud and his
people were out of food and ammunition.

"We were moving every hour from cave to cave. Massoud looked
at the sky and said, 'After we kick the Soviets out of Afghanistan, I
will prepare a loya jirga (council of elders) and form a new democratic government.'"

Junger credits Massoud with a ferocious intellect that shone
through language barriers. He loved talking about ideas. His range
of interests ran from poetry to what went wrong in Rwanda.

Massoud's inner peace came from Islam, says diplomat Amin. He
was a pious individual who prayed five times a day. He had an acute
sense of connecting with God.

That faith helped win him trust, notes Amin. The people gave
him his position because he was a just man. The local peasants were
the source of his support.

His troops were loyal to him because he put them first and
protected them, Amin says. When he chose fighters, he would
weed out those who were fathers of small children, newlyweds or
only sons.

The soldiers would eat first, before officers. Every fighter had a
uniform, soap, toothpaste, boots, shoe polish and monthly pay. He
ran seminars and gave them lectures on guerrilla warfare.

Massoud knew intelligence was key to success, says Amin. He
compared it to the nervous system of the body. His troops learned why
the French lost at Dien Bien Phu, the weaknesses of Che Guevara and
how Mao succeeded on the Long March.

With a look, he could grasp your mind in such a way that you
paid attention. He was quick to respond to questions. He could delegate, and he always tried to avoid casualties.

"He had incredible moral authority," said Reza. He refused to let
his troops smoke cigarettes or hashish.

While many Afghan leaders committed human rights abuses,
only one critical report exists on Massoud, notes Michael Griffin,
British author of "Reaping the Whirlwind: The Taliban Movement
in Afghanistan."

Massoud wouldn't let his men mistreat their enemies, says Reza. His moral authority extended into the heat of battle. He told them, "Never beat a prisoner."

A committee began collecting signatures in January 2004 to have the Nobel Peace Prize awarded to Massoud. Signatories include Czech President Vaclav Havel and American writer Elie Wiesel.

22

Gen. Ulysses S. Grant
His True Grit Helped End The Civil War

Ulysses S. Grant hated war. But when he thought something was necessary, he approached it matter-of-factly.

"The art of war is simple enough. Find out where your enemy is. Get at him as soon as you can. Strike him hard as you can, as often as you can and keep moving on," Grant said.

Following that strategy, then-Brig. Gen. Grant and his army gave the Union its first major victories of the Civil War: Fort Henry and Fort Donelson in February 1862.

When Confederate troops at the latter requested surrender terms, Grant responded firmly: "No terms. Only unconditional and immediate surrender can be accepted."

In April 1862, Grant's army suffered heavy casualties and fell back two miles after the first bloody day at the Battle of Shiloh. The situation was bleak enough to prompt one of his officers to ask if they should make preparations for retreat.

"Retreat? No, I proposed to attack at daylight and whip them," Grant replied, as quoted in "Ulysses S. Grant on Leadership: Executive Lessons from the Front Lines," by John Barnes.

By late afternoon of the next day, it was the Confederate army that was withdrawing. Grant (1822–85) had engineered "one of the most remarkable turnabouts in American military history," Barnes wrote. But a costly price was paid: 13,700 casualties.

Aiming To Win

Even though Grant inflicted far more casualties in four battles than he took, his detractors urged his biggest admirer, President Abraham Lincoln, to relieve him of command.

"I cannot spare this man," Lincoln said. "He fights."

Lincoln had suffered commanding generals such as George McClellan, who seemingly wouldn't fight; Joseph Hooker, whose humiliating retreat following his defeat at Chancellorsville embarrassed Lincoln; and George Meade, who incensed Lincoln by not pursuing Robert E. Lee's army after the Battle of Gettysburg.

Grant was dedicated to winning. Lincoln saw that trait and in March 1864 promoted him to lieutenant general, the country's first since George Washington. He gave Grant command of all the Union armies.

Confederate Gen. James Longstreet, a close friend of Grant before the war, knew what to expect: "That man (Grant) will fight us every day of every hour until the end of this war," he said.

To streamline command, Grant immediately unified the movements of the 19 Union armies under him. Before, they'd sometimes acted independently. Strategic objectives such as territory were essentially replaced with one objective: destruction of all Confederate armies.

The end came a little more than a year later. On April 9, 1865, at Appomattox Courthouse, Va., Grant accepted Lee's surrender of the Army of Northern Virginia, essentially ending the war and restoring the Union.

The images from Appomattox are stirring: "(Lee) the tall, dignified, resplendent aristocrat from Virginia's finest family surrendering to (Grant) the mud-spattered son of a Midwestern tannery owner. This is the stuff of the American dream — the underdog scrambling to the top of the heap," wrote Al Kaltman in "Cigars, Whiskey & Winning: Leadership Lessons from Gen. Ulysses S. Grant."

"Grant is the greatest soldier of our time if not all time," said Union Gen. William T. Sherman. "He fixes in his mind what is the true objective and abandons all minor ones. If his plan goes wrong he is never disconcerted, but promptly devises a new one, and is sure to win in the end."

"I have carefully searched the military records of both ancient and modern history and have never found Grant's superior as a general," said Lee.

Grant, a West Point graduate, distinguished himself in the Mexican War. After resigning his Army commission in 1854, he failed in several occupations. But he stayed positive and had the "inestimable value," Barnes wrote, of the love and support of his wife, Julia. She told all that her husband was destined for great things.

He was 39 years old and working as a clerk in his father's Galena, Ill., leather goods store when the Civil War broke out in 1861. Four years later he was called the "second Father of the Country." In 1868, he was elected the 18th U.S. president.

When the war began, Grant volunteered. But he wanted to serve where he thought he'd do the most good — in a position of responsibility. He persisted in seeking a commission. Finally, five months after the war started, Congress voted him the rank of brigadier general.

Grant stayed modest and humble even as his fame and reputation grew. He made it a point to praise his subordinates and give them all the credit for what was achieved.

"From the beginning of the conflict, winning the war was Grant's only concern — not politics, not personalities, not ambition and certainly not vanity. Except for the intense lobbying effort he undertook in the spring of 1861 to get back into the Army, he did not put himself forward for high-ranking posts, but waited to be noticed," Barnes wrote.

Grant modeled himself after Gen. Zachary Taylor, under whom he'd served in Mexico. Grant admired Taylor because he didn't make demands of his superiors, but made do with what he had and accepted responsibility. It was those same traits that Lincoln came to admire in Grant.

Before making battle decisions, Grant consulted his subordinates. When he heard that Maj. Gen. Phil Sheridan had a plan to attack Confederate positions but was reluctant to present it, Grant sent for him.

"The result was the successful Battle of Five Forks on April 1, 1865, the clash that ultimately unhinged the Confederacy," Barnes wrote.

Grant expected his subordinates to be specific with their facts when presenting plans and did the same in return. He was clear and concise verbally and with written orders, and made certain his subordinates "knew exactly what he wanted, and why, and when he wanted it," according to Barnes.

Grant treated his men with courtesy and respect. "He would not tolerate gossip or backbiting, never swore, and was careful not to chide a subordinate in public and in general tried to command by encouragement rather than reproof," Barnes wrote.

He treated the defeated Confederates with compassion. At Appomattox, his surrender terms exempted all Confederate officers from charges such as treason, provided they took an oath of allegiance to the U.S.

"What is the lesson of Grant's life?" asked President Theodore Roosevelt. "Foremost of all is the lesson of tenacity."

23

Czech Leader
Vaclav Havel
Dissident Writer Dedicated
His Life And Words
To Political Change

Vaclav Havel was just an unknown 20-year-old student in 1956, but he knew his own mind. He didn't like communism.

When he was invited to a three-day conference of young writers held under the Communist Party's auspices in Dobris, Czechoslovakia, though, Havel went.

He went with the intention of speaking out against government censorship. But he realized he was within the bosom of the party. How could he express his real opinion among a room full of famous authors, editors and journalists, all of them members of the party?

When none of the other writers chose to speak first, Havel acted on his instinct to approach everything honestly. He shocked everyone by raising his hand, standing up and speaking out passionately about censorship.

Although the speech he gave was as much criticized as praised, Havel had opened the door to a debate on censorship.

"Since they'd invited me and were putting me up for three days, I felt I had to take advantage of the situation and tell them plainly what I had against them," said Havel in "Vaclav Havel: Disturbing the Peace," by Karel Hvizdala. "It would have been shameful to accept their invitation and remain silent."

His resolve to stay true to himself saw Havel soon becoming one of the most outspoken opponents of communist rule and a leader of dissident groups in Czechoslovakia. After the fall of communism in the Velvet Revolution of November 1989, Havel's efforts led him to become the country's president. In 1993, after the country divided into Czech and Slovak Republics, he became the first president of the Czech Republic. He retired from government in 2003 after his second five-year term.

Voracious Reader

Although the communist system made it hard for him to get the schooling he wanted, Havel was loath to give up on his dream to learn. He got a high school education by attending night school while working as a lab technician by day.

To further his learning, Havel searched for books banned by the government that he knew would be necessary for a balanced education. Knowing that university libraries contained literature not available to the general public, Havel coaxed the librarians into lending him books even though he wasn't a student. When he read a book by a Czech author that interested him, he would immediately seek out the author to question him or her firsthand.

Havel was inspired enough by what he read that he began writing as well. But his audience seemed limited to him.

Realizing the potential for theater to inspire individuals to question the communist regime, Havel soon began writing plays, beginning with "The Garden Party" in 1963.

Aware of the danger of censors — he'd seen other writers imprisoned for their honesty about communism — Havel used wit and a sense of the absurd to criticize the government subtly. To gain the sympathy of the audience, he appealed to common truths and morals he felt were absent under the communists. Then, to keep the audience thinking about those themes, he encouraged discussion between actors and spectators long after a performance was over.

Aware of the importance of international support, he traveled outside the country, exchanging ideas with exiles and drumming up support with foreign media.

Then Havel witnessed the brutality of the Soviets when they invaded to put down the brief flowering of Czechoslovakian freedom in the "Prague Spring" of 1968. Repulsed at the beatings and killings of so many unarmed Czechs, Havel vowed to work for political change. He said he would do whatever it took to get it.

"It is impossible to write about great causes without living for those great causes, to be a great poet without being a great human being," Havel said. "Man must discover again, within himself, a deeper sense of responsibility toward the world, which means responsibility toward something higher than himself."

To gain insight into the Communist Party, Havel made friends with carefully chosen politicians in Prague who kept him informed of important news.

Havel knew he'd have to make the best of difficult situations in order to succeed. When he discovered his apartment was bugged in 1968, he immediately called a dozen journalists to his home. Then, to give them the juiciest scoop, Havel called over the police and engaged them about the bugging while the reporters secretly took it all down from the next room.

Despite increasing censorship and restrictions on his activities, Havel kept up his fight. When his writings were blacklisted and authorities began to withhold his royalties from abroad, Havel worked in a brewery to make ends meet. Although many anti-communist Czech writers left the country to publish abroad, Havel chose to stay to urge others to fight from within. He even turned down offers by foreign organizations to pay him to write plays abroad.

Co-writing a human-rights declaration called "Charter 77" in 1977 — to inspire all to democracy — landed him in jail from 1979 until 1984, but Havel refused to give in to persecution.

In 1989, he helped found a new opposition group called "Civic Forum." Convinced that a revolutionary movement must have broad-based appeal to succeed, Havel sought out Czechs from every social level — communists and non-communists alike — to sign his petitions for democratic reform.

"He united people who held different opinions and gave them a joint program," wrote Eda Kriseova in "Vaclav Havel: The Authorized Biography." "(He) was always pushing everything further, into unfamiliar territory, where no one had yet dared to go."

To gain the upper hand in debates with defenders of communism, Havel limited his discussion to facts. Instead of challenging one ideology with another, Havel talked of real-world problems where he knew he had the advantage because communist policies had failed.

Keen Negotiator

Once he became a voice for the freedom movement, Havel was called upon to negotiate between workers and party members. During such sessions, Havel focused on specific goals and didn't get sidetracked into vague ideological debates.

"(It's) a thousand times more valuable to insist, regardless of the consequences, on something more modest but realistic," said Havel, "than to pacify one's conscience by firing off loudmouthed proposals that evaporate (the moment they're made)."

During negotiations, Havel believed that each concession gained would help lead to further concessions later on. He refused to give in, therefore, even on the smallest points he thought were important, while staying focused on his broader goals.

"Don't get mixed up in backroom wheeling and dealing," Havel said. "And be prepared to stick to your guns in the end."

His approach entranced the Czechs, and they pushed him to run for office after Czechoslovakia was freed from communist domination. He agreed, but he decided he would run his campaign his way — humbly.

Havel often broke his schedule to chat with people in cafes and bars to get their input and opinions. Convinced that good communication led to good government, he was as eager to talk with political adversaries as foreign heads of state. Placing little emphasis on stuffy etiquette, Havel pushed for an informal atmosphere within his administration.

Havel suffered a lisp, and to prevent himself from appearing slow or uninformed, he memorized every detail of his speeches. He won over listeners by showing he was solidly informed.

Although the causes Havel fought for concerned the welfare of millions, he stressed that it's crucial to enjoy oneself in order to keep a balance.

"You don't want to dissolve in your own seriousness to the point where you become ridiculous to everyone," said Havel. "Without the laughter, it would be impossible to do serious things."

24

Liberator
Toussaint L'Ouverture
His Drive For Freedom
Charted The Path
To Haiti's Independence

It was 1793 in St. Domingue, now known as Haiti. French rulers had just promised freedom to the island's slave population as a way of ending two years of armed revolt.

François-Dominique Toussaint a Bréda, a former slave and leader of the revolt, sensed the promise would be empty. But how would he convince his fellow slaves?

Realizing that freedom was the common goal, he circulated a letter among the slaves telling them he'd lead them to it. He urged them to fight alongside him instead of trusting proven enemies.

Then, to give himself the air of authority, he signed the letter, "Toussaint L'Ouverture," French for "Toussaint the Opener."

By keeping his goal of freedom simple, Toussaint (1746–1803) soon was able to command the strength and respect of thousands of slaves and Frenchmen. His leadership in the decade following the initial 1791 uprising brought about independence for Haiti in the years after his death and served as an inspiration to thousands of colonists the world over.

"I was born a slave, but nature gave me a soul of a free man," Toussaint was quoted as saying in "Toussaint L'Ouverture," by Thomas and Dorothy Hoobler.

Knowledge Is Power

Although education for slaves in St. Domingue was strictly forbidden, young Toussaint saw that learning was the key to advancing. He lobbied his godfather, Pierre Baptiste, to teach him. Baptiste taught the youth to read and speak French in addition to the Creole spoken by slaves.

When an overseer offered Toussaint books from a library, he jumped at the chance. The young slave spent his free time reading everything he was given, including the military histories of Julius Caesar and Alexander the Great.

When the slaves' revolt began on Aug. 22, 1791, Toussaint, then nearly 50, joined the rebels. Putting his life's accumulated knowledge to use, Toussaint first applied his skills as a field doctor. Before long, he was advising the leaders, drawing on his familiarity with European military campaigns.

Soon he was given a command of troops. Toussaint analyzed their strengths and weaknesses and saw that to succeed, the rebels would need a morale boost and more discipline.

So he spent time with them, listening to and then addressing their concerns. To make them better fighters, he drilled them in the fashion of European armies, stressing organized attack over senseless charges.

Toussaint knew that his men couldn't achieve more unless the basics — food, clothing and shelter — also were taken care of. To feed his troops, he ordered an end to the burning of overthrown plantations and encouraged the replanting of sugarcane.

Knowing that an army needed stability, not wild excess, he punished his own soldiers when he found them abusing captured prisoners.

Aware that his troops still were no match for the well-trained French, Toussaint devised alternate tactics. By combining the maneuverability of his soldiers with a knowledge of the terrain, he became one of the first commanders to employ guerrilla warfare, according to "'This Gilded African,' Toussaint L'Ouverture," by Wenda Parkinson.

To strengthen his position, he searched for allies. He soon enlisted the support of Spain, which controlled Santo Domingo, the eastern part of the island. With Spain's aid, Toussaint now had a ready supply of arms with which to battle the French.

Although the French soundly defeated him in initial encounters, Toussaint didn't get discouraged. He gathered his forces in Santo Domingo and planned to regroup.

Toussaint knew the importance of reliable commanders, so he surrounded himself with the officers he trusted most. To build public regard for his cause, he instructed his men not to harm civilians and to leave captured villages intact.

When word spread of the rebels' restraint in using force, many villagers surrendered readily. Thousands joined the uprising in a matter of months, including a number of French officers.

To get the most out of his men, Toussaint led by example. He worked tirelessly, often getting by on only two hours of sleep a night.

Peacetime Solutions

His resolve paid off. After a number of victories, Toussaint had the French on the ropes. Sensing the enemy was vulnerable, he decided the time was ripe for negotiation. Waiting until after the French government freed its slaves in February 1794, Toussaint soon accepted an offer to end the fighting.

There were still problems after peace with the French. Freed slaves, now known as "cultivators," often revolted in the face of continued hard work.

Realizing the benefit of a good slogan, he pinched one from the French Revolution. Proclaiming the cause of "Liberty, Equality, Fraternity," Toussaint urged the cultivators to go back to work.

"Liberty cannot exist without work," he told them.

Now that the fighting was over, the first goal was to restore order. Toussaint knew he'd need the cooperation of all groups. He urged blacks, whites and mulattoes to work together for the common good.

To emphasize his point, he used dramatic flair. During a public speech, he lifted two bottles of wine, one red and one white, and poured them together to show they made one color.

Knowing a solid infrastructure was necessary to maintain progress, Toussaint began rebuilding the war-torn country. He invited priests and artists to teach in the schools. To give the people pleasure, he built a theater. To impress visitors, he built a hotel.

He strengthened his ties with people by taking time to see them personally. He rode to plantations to make sure cultivators were being paid. He dropped in at schools to hear students recite lessons.

When he declared his country independent from France in 1801, however, Napoleon sent a large force to retake it. Overwhelmed, Toussaint had to surrender. He was imprisoned in France until his death.

But he never gave up the battle for freedom.

"In overthrowing me, you have cut down . . . only the trunk of the tree of liberty," he said to his captors. "It will spring up again from the roots, for there are many and they are deep."

He was right. Within three years, the remaining resistance drove out the French and formed Haiti on Jan. 1, 1804.

25

Statesman
Nelson Mandela
He Persevered Against
Apartheid — And Won

Nelson Rolihlahla Mandela had a problem. One of the clients in his law practice was a black woman employed as a housekeeper by a white family. His client was accused of stealing her employer's clothes. In apartheid-ruled South Africa, Mandela's black client stood little chance of winning acquittal from an all-white jury.

He analyzed his options. He made sure he knew the relevant case law inside and out. Then he decided to pour on the drama.

"I did not act as though I were a black man in a white man's court, but as if everyone else — white and black — was a guest in my court," he recalled in his autobiography, "Long Walk to Freedom." "When trying a case, I often made sweeping gestures and used high-flown language."

During the trial, he hammered away at holes in the employer's story. As a finale, he walked over to a table where some of the allegedly stolen clothing was displayed. He cautiously poked at the pile and then used the tip of his pencil to pick up a woman's undergarment. Looking steadily at the accuser, he held it out and asked, "Madam, are these . . . yours?"

Too embarrassed to admit ownership, the woman denied it. Mandela's strategy worked, and the magistrate dismissed the case.

Faces Fears

That ability to confront issues helped Mandela become South Africa's first black president and one of the men credited with bringing peace to a nation that had been torn by racial strife for more than 300 years.

But he wasn't always comfortable in the spotlight. In his early 20s, Mandela feared speaking in public. He knew that if he were going to influence anyone, he'd have to overcome the problem.

He faced his fear and forced himself to address large groups at civil-liberties rallies. He'd focus on the problem of racism and forget his anxiety. Soon, he found himself able to stand in front of thousands of people and speak comfortably.

Mandela, born July 18, 1918, pursued his goals tirelessly. He realized as a youth that education was key to success. Even though he was a poor student in grade school, he improved steadily "not so much through cleverness as through doggedness," he wrote.

The first in his family to go to college, Mandela studied law at South Africa's prestigious Witwatersrand University and the University of South Africa. He saw that South Africa had no black law firm in the early 1950s — so he opened the first one, in Johannesburg.

"To reach our offices each morning, we had to move through a crowd of people in the hallways, on the stairs and in our small waiting room," Mandela said.

To fight legalized racism, Mandela united blacks, Indians and those of mixed race in the Campaign for the Defiance of Unjust Laws in 1952. To make sure the campaign gained worldwide attention, he meticulously planned a two-stage program.

"In the first stage, a small number of well-trained volunteers would break selected laws in a handful of urban areas," he said. "They would enter proscribed areas without permits, use whites-only facilities such as toilets, railway compartments, waiting rooms and post office entrances. They would deliberately remain in town after curfew."

Yet Mandela knew that South African whites might try to ignore the protesters. To ensure they didn't, he told supporters that they needed to practice "mass defiance, accompanied by strikes."

The process was repeated region by region over five months. The landmark five-month campaign raised world awareness of apartheid and increased membership in the African National Congress (ANC) — the civil-liberties group founded in 1912 — from 20,000 to 100,000.

Mandela saw the ANC's growth as an opportunity to bring even more unity. In 1955, he organized the Congress of the People to unite the country's anti-apartheid forces and "create a set of principles . . . for a new South Africa." More than 3,000 delegates attended the congress, including 112 whites. The convention adopted the landmark Freedom Charter, a set of democratic principles that "endorsed private enterprise and would allow capitalism to flourish among Africans," Mandela said.

He'd always believed in democracy, learning about it from the tribal chief who raised him in the rural town of Mqhekezweni after his father died. The chief held tribal meetings in which "everyone was heard, chief and subject, warrior and medicine man, shopkeeper and farmer," Mandela recalled. People spoke without interruption.

Mandela disliked violence, and he urged supporters to follow Indian organizer Mohandas Gandhi's principles of peaceful protest. He didn't shy away from self-defense, though. When South African police met nonviolence with violence, the ANC "had no choice but to change course," he said.

Even when the South African government imprisoned him for involvement with the ANC and other banned civil-liberties groups, Mandela refused to give up. He persevered during 27 years in prison, constantly trying to alert the world to the injustices that took place.

He understood the value of public relations. Mandela staged hunger strikes and issued messages through his lawyer and others allowed to visit him. He'd also issue statements telling the world about the political imprisonment of government opponents, torture and legal racism.

As other African countries and Western democracies distanced themselves from South Africa, the government made repeated offers to set Mandela free — if he renounced his position.

He held his ground. "I responded that the state was responsible for the violence — that it is always the oppressor, not the oppressed, who dictates the form of the struggle," Mandela said. "It was not up to us to renounce violence, but the government."

He quickly became a world-renowned symbol of South Africa's oppression. By the late 1980s, his fierce determination had helped persuade other countries — including the U.S. — to impose sweeping sanctions against South Africa until the government agreed to recognize all ethnic groups as citizens with full rights.

Finally, South Africa President P.W. Botha agreed to see Mandela.

Mandela threw himself into negotiations. He spent hours with Botha and his successor, F.W. de Klerk, laying out the ANC's demands for a new South Africa. He urged them to lift the ban on the ANC and other civil-liberties groups and end the state of emergency that gave police sweeping powers. He also urged the release of political prisoners and demanded that exiles be allowed to return to South Africa.

On Feb. 2, 1990, six months after taking office, de Klerk agreed to most of Mandela's demands. Nine days later, Mandela was released from prison.

Keep It Moving

But the struggle wasn't over. During the next four years, Mandela helped lead negotiations to set up a democratic South Africa. The country held its first multiracial elections in April 1994.

Opinion polls showed the ANC had a sizable majority. Still, Mandela and other party officials worked as though they faced an uphill battle.

"The task was a formidable one," Mandela said. "We estimated there would be (more than) 20 million people going to the polls, most of them voting for the first time. Many of our voters were illiterate and likely to be intimidated by the mere idea of voting."

To reach those who couldn't read, Mandela and others trained more than 100,000 people to assist with voter registration. ANC candidates traveled the country holding meetings — called "people's forums" — in villages and towns to listen "to the hopes and fears, the ideas and complaints, of our people." These responses helped the party form its platform.

The ANC won 62.6% of the national vote and 252 of 400 seats in the National Assembly. Mandela took office as president May 10, 1994.

For efforts in ending apartheid, Mandela, with de Klerk, received the Nobel Peace Prize in 1993.

In 1999, Mandela stepped down as president to make way for Thabo Mbeki, who was nominated ANC president in 1997. After

Mandela's retirement from government, he continued traveling the world, meeting leaders, attending conferences and collecting awards.

He remains especially passionate about the impact of AIDS on South Africa, as emphasized in his 2004 farewell speech to Parliament. Mandela also created the Nelson Mandela Children's Fund to care for children from impoverished backgrounds to improve the quality of their lives.

26

Sitting Bull
A Warrior Only By Necessity

The measure of a leader is character. And Sioux tribal elders believed they had a good way to take that measurement.

Lakota Sioux warrior Sitting Bull wanted to be a chief. But so did another young rival.

So tribal elders chose a very handsome warrior "to go tell each that he'd stolen their wife," said Ron His Horse Is Thunder, a great-great-great grandson of Sitting Bull.

Each had a choice. Under Sioux custom, stealing another man's wife was a terrible crime. The victim could choose to kill the offender. And that's what the first candidate wanted to do.

"He immediately grabbed his rifle and went after the handsome young warrior," said His Horse Is Thunder. "He chased him through camp and created quite a disturbance."

The fight was stopped before it'd gone too far. Then Sitting Bull was told the same story. "Sitting Bull instantly offered the young man his horse and blankets and other things needed to survive on the plains," said His Horse Is Thunder. "He told the man he should take those possessions. He wanted his wife to be well taken care of."

The tribe's elders saw that Sitting Bull put his jealousy aside to maintain harmony in the camp — and put his wife's welfare above his own. As a result, Sitting Bull's stature grew, and he became chief.

With similar thoughtful, measured and brave actions, Sitting Bull (circa 1831–90) became one of the greatest American Indian leaders and a key figure in America's growth.

As explorers and hunters moved west, bands of white settlers clashed with Indians over culture and land. That struggle put Sitting Bull in the middle of the 19th century's biggest economic expansion.

Fighting U.S. troops wasn't his intention. "All he wanted was for his people to be left alone," said His Horse Is Thunder. "He didn't see any honor in fighting the white man."

Victory was hollow without honor to Sitting Bull, says His Horse Is Thunder, who serves as president of Sitting Bull College.

"Anyone could shoot a rifle — that didn't seem like an act of courage to Sitting Bull," said His Horse Is Thunder. "And that's what battle was for in his eyes. A life-and-death struggle should reward those with the most courage to act on their convictions."

Sitting Bull set about to prove himself early. At age 14, he'd already absorbed the lessons of his father and other warriors, learning the ins and outs of battle. He sparred with other boys to become a better fighter, and through endless practice he learned to throw a spear and shoot to hit his mark the first time.

As a teen, he led war parties into combat. On horseback with arrows flying past him, he'd charge right into the fray.

Hands-On Warrior

His strategy wasn't to try for an immediate victory. Sitting Bull avoided swinging knives and tomahawks, and instead grabbed his opponent on the arm or head to trounce his confidence.

"You couldn't do anything much braver than to attack an armed enemy with a bare hand," said Greg Gagnon, a professor of Indian studies at the University of North Dakota. "It was a way to show dominance over an enemy."

Sitting Bull matched his bravery with a sense of community — sharing built greater loyalty. "He gave almost everything he didn't need away," said Gagnon.

Sitting Bull believed strongly that there was a divine power and that it was just. Members of his tribe considered him a prophet. "He was a warrior because he had to be," Gagnon said, "but he was also very spiritual."

Soon, Indians from all around came to his camp to join him, making him one of the greatest leaders among the Northern Plains Indians.

That led to an unprecedented coalition of tribes. At its zenith, the Sioux territory stretched from Montana to Minnesota. Divided into three main tribes, each was identified by different dialects.

Then gold was discovered in the Lakota territories in South Dakota's Black Hills in 1874. A huge land rush ensued.

Sitting Bull's people watched as even the most basic of resources became scarce. Within two years, tribes were fighting one another as well as settlers from the East Coast.

The U.S. Army dispatched troops to the Lakota territories to safeguard the growing camps of miners. In 1876, soldiers attacked Sitting Bull's camp. They were repelled. To protect the tribe and avoid another raid, Sitting Bull ordered the tribe to move. But a young lieutenant colonel, George Custer, found Sitting Bull's new camp 10 days later.

"He was under orders to wait for his commanding general before taking any action," said His Horse Is Thunder. "But Custer decided to attack anyway."

Sitting Bull anticipated such a decision, and he was prepared. He'd already persuaded several thousand Lakotas — representing at least four major tribes — to unite. That had never happened.

A quarter of the Indians gathered were well-trained warriors. Even though he was in his mid-40s — elderly for a plains warrior — they submitted to Sitting Bull's command.

Sitting Bull had chosen those with good strategic skills to lead each flank of his warriors. He also made sure he had swift riders with him and his deputies. That let him stay up on the hills overlooking Little Bighorn in Montana, where he could best direct the battle and send messages.

Winning Attitude

The Army's troops were much better armed. Yet knowing that attitude is half the battle in any challenge, Sitting Bull told his people he was confident they'd win. His assurance boosted morale.

"His vision went unquestioned," said His Horse Is Thunder. "His warriors never doubted they'd pull off one of the biggest military victories of the 19th century."

Which they did, annihilating more than 200 troops of the 7th Cavalry. So humiliated were leaders in Washington, D.C., by the defeat, they chased Sitting Bull to Canada.

Within five years, his tribe was suffering from hunger and disease. To save it, Sitting Bull surrendered to government troops and was thrown into a military prison in Nebraska. Two years later, he was released to join his people at Standing Rock Reservation, which straddled both Dakotas.

He grew weary of life on a reservation. Seeking challenges, he asked for and received permission to join Buffalo Bill Cody's Wild West Show, traveling around the world.

Sitting Bull was amazed at the number of beggars on the streets of some of Europe's biggest cities. To raise money to help the needy he saw, the Indian chief started selling autographs. He then gave away all of the money he made to the homeless. And when world leaders came to greet him in his travels, he turned their gifts over to the less fortunate. He kept nothing for himself.

"Sitting Bull gave Indians a real hero, someone to look up to even today," said Gagnon. "He was much more than a great warrior. He was a great man who came to symbolize the best qualities of Indian culture."

27

First Lady
Eleanor Roosevelt

Her Dedication To Helping Others
Made History

Being born into one of New York's oldest and most respected families might sound like a ticket to the carefree life, but that wasn't the case for Eleanor Roosevelt.

The child of an alcoholic father and a beautiful, socialite mother who teased her plain-faced daughter with nicknames like "Granny," Eleanor was shot with insecurity and orphaned by age 10.

She would overcome her history to become the most influential first lady in American history and a charter delegate to the United Nations.

Roosevelt (1884–1962) started making progress almost immediately. While she lived with her strict maternal grandmother, Roosevelt spent much time with her aunts and uncles, visiting the theater and reading books.

Roosevelt loved reading, and steeped herself in books. She was heavily influenced by what she read and learned.

Her friend and biographer, Joseph Lash, wrote in "Eleanor and Franklin" that by age 14, "Eleanor had definite opinions, was reflective, and was capable of a crisp expression of her views. . . . She wanted to succeed."

At age 15, Eleanor went to school in England, where she met the teacher who would become her role model: Marie Souvestre. Lash wrote that a former student said Souvestre was so gifted "in exciting, amusing, in passionately interesting the intellect . . . that it seemed as if we could never think anything dull again."

Souvestre was also concerned about politics and social policies. For three years, Eleanor was motivated by this dynamic teacher, leaving school only because her grandmother insisted she get back for cotillion season.

When she returned to the U.S., Roosevelt knew that she wanted more than the courting and society mingling expected of young, upper-class girls. Lash wrote that "all she wished for was to do something useful: that was her main object."

By age 20, Roosevelt was doing just that. Far from the typical high-society debutante, concerned solely with dances and potential husbands, she was actively involved in organizations devoted to the working poor. She took the public bus alone into some of New York City's worst slums.

This hands-on involvement was shocking to many from her well-bred background. Even so, it set the stage for the rest of her public life.

Roosevelt's gumption also impressed her distant cousin and future husband, Franklin Delano Roosevelt. Unlike most society belles, she had substance, and FDR wanted to marry her.

Putting aside her own hopes to become a teacher — "respectable" married women didn't work outside their homes — Roosevelt married Franklin. Uncle Theodore, then the U.S. president, gave her away at the wedding.

But it wasn't her dream. "I do not think that I am a natural-born mother," she wrote years later.

Still, she was always there for her family. She raised five children and, until FDR entered politics in 1910, bore the undue influence of her ever-present mother-in-law, who controlled FDR's inheritance.

Overcoming Obstacles

That challenge wasn't her biggest. That would come when she discovered her husband had an affair with her secretary. Determined to heal, the 34-year-old Roosevelt pushed herself back into volunteering.

Two years later, inspired by the suffragists who finally achieved the vote for women in 1920, she joined the League of Women Voters.

There she developed strong friendships with progressive, public-minded women who encouraged her to become more active in politics and vocal on social issues.

With two of these women, she co-founded a girls' school. Later, the three started a furniture business.

Lash wrote that Roosevelt was at first no gifted speaker. She had a nervous giggle that critics liked to point out. She kept at it, though, and learned to speak effectively by imagining her listeners' problems and concerns as she spoke to them. This technique gave her words power, and she became one of the most popular speakers in the country.

According to Doris Kearns Goodwin in "No Ordinary Time," Eleanor Roosevelt's speech at the 1940 Democratic Convention — the first time the wife of a presidential nominee spoke at a major political party gathering — managed to calm the rivalries of a party whose leader was going to break the two-term presidential precedent.

Roosevelt kept herself busy; to keep herself organized, she carefully wrote down all her appointments in her planner. A typical day she once outlined for her readers started at 6:45 a.m. and ended at 1:30 a.m. And her work ethic showed in her productivity.

Roosevelt's writing output alone was astounding. Allida Black, editor of "Courage in a Dangerous World," wrote that Roosevelt's production totaled four autobiographies, seven scholarly essays, seven children's books, more than 550 articles, more than 100,000 letters, a monthly column for 30 years and a five-day-a-week column for 27 years.

When World War II brought millions of mothers into the work force, Roosevelt became a relentless advocate of child care in the workplace. Finally, she convinced Kaiser shipyards to create a model day care, the success of which, according to Goodwin, "stimulated war plants and shipyards across the nation to provide day care."

By the end of the war, wrote Goodwin, more than 1.5 million children were in day care.

Every Soldier Counts

Knowing the importance of communication, Roosevelt went all out in her public visits. When she visited American soldiers wounded in the Pacific, she walked bed to bed, grabbed every soldier's hand and asked what he needed. When soldiers asked that she call their loved ones, she did.

"After talking to almost 400,000 men during her five-week visit to 17 islands in the Pacific, she brought home four fat notebooks filled with names and addresses of mothers and girlfriends," wrote Rochelle Chadakoff, editor of "Eleanor Roosevelt's My Day."

Determined to bring equality to all people, Roosevelt served as a pioneer in shedding official light on civil rights.

In 1936, she invited black opera singer Marian Anderson to perform at the White House. Three years later, when Anderson was denied a performance at Constitution Hall, Roosevelt arranged an open-air concert on the steps of the Lincoln Memorial. More than 75,000 people attended.

She continued trying to erase color barriers. In 1943, Roosevelt was outraged after reading a letter from a black Army sergeant about the morale-shattering segregated facilities at his base. She began a letter-writing campaign so intense that it helped trigger a War Department directive within a few days.

All signs designating any recreational facilities "White" or "Colored only" were ordered removed from all military sites. Goodwin wrote, "It was a beginning wedge in the desegregation of the armed forces."

Throughout her life, Roosevelt remained humble. She said in Russell Freedman's "Eleanor Roosevelt: A Life of Discovery," "About the only value the story of my life may have is to show that one can, even without any particular gifts, overcome obstacles that seem insurmountable if one is willing to face the fact that they must be overcome; that, in spite of timidity and fear, in spite of a lack of special talents, one can find a way to live widely and fully."

PART 4

Innovation And Strategy Drive Their Success

©Bettmann/CORBIS

There is no saying to what length an enterprising man may push his good fortune.

> — GEORGE WASHINGTON TO THE
> NEW YORK COUNCIL OF SAFETY,
> PHILADELPHIA, AUGUST 4, 1777
> (IN "THE QUOTABLE GEORGE WASHINGTON,"
> ED. STEPHEN LUCAS)

28

Alexander The Great
This Innovative Strategist
Inspired His Soldiers
To Conquer An Empire

When inhabitants of the Phoenician island of Tyre refused to concede in 333 B.C., Alexander the Great knew he needed to stage an invasion.

But Phoenicians were the world's best sailors at the time. Alexander knew his weaknesses, and ocean warfare was one of them.

No matter. When one has big aims, one thinks big, too. Alexander ordered his army to build a causeway 2,000 feet long by 200 feet wide from the mainland to the island.

"He practiced an 'economy of losses,'" said Frank Holt, history professor at the University of Houston and author of "Alexander the Great and Bactria."

"He made sure he achieved what he wanted with a minimum of losses to his forces. That brought him a great deal of support," Holt said.

Building his land bridge took seven months. All the while, Alexander's troops labored under enemy fire. But after years of fighting for him, knowing he made decisions with his focus on triumph, they kept on.

They transformed the island of Tyre into a peninsula and took it for their own. Today, deep beneath Tyre's asphalt streets and apartment buildings, remnants of Alexander's improbable highway remain.

Before his death at age 32, Alexander the Great (356–323 B.C.), heir to the Macedonian throne, consolidated an empire that covered 1 million square miles — from Gibraltar to the Punjab. He founded more than 70 cities, became leader of the Greeks, pharaoh of Egypt and king of Asia. He was more powerful than any other leader of his time.

He acted as if he knew no fear. "On some occasions, he bordered on reckless," Holt said.

Take how he once lured opposing forces into a trap. Alexander entered battle wearing magnificent armor and a white-winged helmet. He was diverting the enemy's attention so that a second wing of his troops could launch a surprise attack. He nearly lost his life in that gambit, according to Richard Stoneman in "Alexander the Great."

At a battle near the Asian river Granicus, Alexander was first to plunge into the water and head for a far bank. On one occasion, he countered flagging morale among his troops by scaling the walls of an enemy Indian city and jumping into the foe's midst, forcing his commanders to rush after him.

Alexander didn't flinch when it came to enduring hardship. Spurred by Greek epic heroes before him, such as Achilles, he fought alongside his men in his army's front line.

In his 13-year military career, Alexander suffered nine serious wounds, including an arrow shot through a lung, a catapult missile hurled through a shoulder and a head injury that nearly blinded him, wrote Eugene Borza in "The Impact of Alexander the Great."

His willingness to do whatever he asked of his men evoked a dedication in them that later leaders, including Caesar and Napoleon, envied.

In the spring of 329 B.C., Alexander led his starving, snow-blinded troops (many of whom were more than 60 years old) across the icy Hindu Kush mountain range in central Asia, a feat of endurance that, historians agree, far surpassed Hannibal's crossing of the Alps, according to Robin Lane Fox in "The Search for Alexander."

Under his command, Alexander's men traveled 20,000 miles and remained away from their families for 12 years. They marched 30 miles a day across deserts in blinding summer heat.

Prior to each battle, Alexander reviewed his troops, conversed with officers, singled out soldiers who'd performed bravely in past battles, and praised their exploits. He's said to have remembered the names of hundreds of men.

After skirmishes, Alexander visited the wounded, congratulated those who distinguished themselves in battle and honored them with gifts of money.

He tolerated no half-hearted efforts from his followers. Those who took exception to the way he led were punished swiftly, often by death.

He was a brilliant strategist. He not only studied military history but he also learned tactics firsthand by observing his father, Philip II of Macedon.

Possessing a supple, imaginative mind, Alexander adapted his military maneuvers to counter the strengths of his foes. He never fought the same battle twice, and he would attack from unexpected directions at unanticipated times.

His insight into how to weaken his foes' resolve helped him trick his enemies into making fatal mistakes. At the Battle of Hydaspes, according to Fox in "The Search for Alexander," he marched his troops every night along the banks of the Hydaspes River (today the Jhelum River in western India and Pakistan), ordering them to blow trumpets and bellow war cries, to provoke his enemy Porus into action.

Every evening, Porus prepared his men for battle, only to witness Alexander's men beat a hasty retreat. This "pas de deux" continued for days until Porus stopped reacting. Then Alexander and his army stole ashore near Porus' camp and decimated Porus' forces.

By 333 B.C., Alexander had conquered western Asia Minor. Two years later, he gained complete control of the eastern Mediterranean coast. He was savvy enough to realize that his political and military opponents weren't personal enemies to be degraded.

To win support of his Persian subjects, he attempted to establish a "common concord" between the Greeks and the Persians, Fox wrote.

He gave the Persians administrative jobs, brought Persian style into his court and even wore their style of clothing — long robe, sash and cape, all in the royal Persian colors. While this won him favor with the Persians, Greeks were furious that he not only was adapting to Persian style but also encouraging them to do so.

While he was politically skilled with those he conquered, he was a poor administrator throughout his reign. Before launching his eastern campaign, Alexander abolished direct taxation in Macedonia to stir support but nearly led the country into bankruptcy. He hired a boyhood friend, Harpalus, as the imperial treasurer, but the unreliable friend embezzled huge sums.

Another serious misjudgment on Alexander's part was his undoing. Pressing through India in torrential rains and mud, he pushed his troops beyond their limits.

He recalled past victories and promised rewards, but his rallying speech failed this time. The men were homesick and refused to go on. A vengeful Alexander led them through enemy territory in a grueling march homeward.

He died soon afterward under mysterious circumstances.

Still, Alexander remains one of history's greatest military leaders. As noted by Peter Green, author of "Alexander of Macedon," he led a life summed up by Tennyson's final line in "Ulysses": "To strive, to seek, to find, and not to yield."

29

President George Washington
Father Of Our Nation Pushed For Success

Most Americans consider George Washington a great citizen. Washington himself thought his efforts were weak compared to those of his older brother, Lawrence.

Lawrence was educated in England, became a successful farmer, married into the landed gentry and served the British army with distinction. These were all things George wanted out of his own life.

George didn't have a formal education or military training. But he didn't let that stand in his way. For Washington (1732–99), success stemmed from emulating those he admired, a constant desire to learn and unceasing industriousness.

Washington's philosophy is summed up in a quote from a play he often used in letters: "'Tis not in mortals to command success. But we'll do more; we'll deserve it."

Washington had to work hard to get anything in life. George expected to follow Lawrence to an English grammar school. But their father's early death scotched those plans.

The estate had to be divided among seven children. Around age 12, George had to drop out of school. Yet he used the education he had to become a land surveyor. By 14, he was surveying land for his brother and other Virginia farmers.

George moved in with Lawrence and his wife, who was related to Lord Fairfax of England. Despite a lack of formal education, Washington decided he could teach himself what he wanted to know. By careful observation and mimicry, he learned to move with ease in these circles by studying the book "Rules of Civility and Decent Behavior."

Young Washington impressed Lord Fairfax and other wealthy Virginians with his manners and industry. Fairfax appointed Washington to survey Virginia and other land Fairfax owned. George was then 17.

Peter Henriques, associate professor of history at George Mason University, says Virginia's slave economy bred laziness and bad manners in some landed gentry. Washington eschewed both.

"Washington's mature, he's responsible, he's diffident around his elders," Henriques said. "These powerful men take a shine to him and help him advance in life."

Washington looked constantly for new responsibilities that would help him grow. When Lawrence died, George lobbied to take over his military commission. With no military training, Washington became a British officer.

The French and Indian War sorely tested Washington's new vocation. Washington relied on his backwoods expertise to help him lead a successful ambush early on, but later he surrendered a fort after a French siege killed a third of his troops.

Even though he gave up his post after the surrender, Washington didn't stay discouraged. He learned from his mistakes, Henriques says, by reading military manuals.

"He's a man who goes to school all the time," Henriques said. "The lack of formal education didn't stop him from learning."

Wasington would hold that determined approach dear for the rest of his life. "There is no saying to what length an enterprising man may push his good fortune," he said in 1777, according to author Stephen Lucas.

He accepted subsequent appointments and served with distinction through the rest of the war. Washington rose from major to commander of the entire Virginia regiment.

The ability to learn from mistakes and try new things carried over to his life as a farmer at Mount Vernon.

He expanded Mount Vernon's land holdings, always looking for the best crops.

Tobacco was the most popular product out of Virginia at the time. All farmers were encouraged to plant it. But Washington thought his tobacco sellers were cheating him. And he noticed tobacco crops weakened the soil.

He studied botanical books, talked to successful planters and began planting other crops such as wheat, oats and corn. He built a distillery and added livestock to the farm. Henriques says Washington was a rock-ribbed realist, interested in becoming more prosperous.

Above all, he sought activity and new experiences. Washington abhorred idleness. "Every hour wasted is lost forever," Washington wrote to his stepson.

Washington's industry helped Mount Vernon become an 8,000-acre farm. If not for the American Revolution, he'd have been content to remain there all his life.

As a distinguished veteran of the French and Indian War, Washington was the natural choice to lead the colonial army. Yet he had reservations. "I do not think myself equal to the command," he told the Continental Congress.

The early Continental Army was a sharp contrast from Washington's experience with trained British soldiers in the French and Indian War. Washington suffered several defeats and retreated numerous times. Yet each time he reviewed his mistakes and vowed not to repeat them.

Washington sometimes was harsh with his troops. He used hangings and beatings to punish deserters and instill discipline. Yet he knew he had to make do with what he had.

"We must make use of the men as we find them," Washington once wrote. "We cannot make them as we wish."

Though steeped in the traditions of the British military, Washington was flexible. For example, he used a hit-and-run approach learned in the French and Indian War.

That tactic was unheard of at a time when soldiers were only supposed to engage the enemy when in strict formation. But hit-and-run raids produced two of Washington's first big victories at Trenton and Princeton, both in New Jersey.

After the war, Washington could say he achieved everything he wanted: glory on the battlefield and success on the farm. But he was called to serve in a third realm, politics.

Again, Washington was reluctant to take the post. He was afraid it would appear to be a power grab. But when elected, Washington threw himself into the role.

Knowing he'd need help, he looked for the brightest minds to guide the fledgling republic. He appointed Alexander Hamilton as the first secretary of the treasury, and the author of the Declaration of Independence, Thomas Jefferson, as secretary of state.

But Washington's appointees, especially Hamilton and Jefferson, were strong-willed and ambitious. Washington had to strike a balance between the two men, who held very different views about the country's political future.

Washington would also go against the people of the U.S. when he thought it was right.

When Britain and France went to war, U.S. citizens wanted to support the old ally, France. Washington knew the new country was still too weak. So he supported neutrality.

Many people, including Jefferson, considered this stance treasonous. But Washington stood his ground and kept America out of war.

Henriques said, "Washington knew that he was the first and everything he would do would set a precedent for the country."

30

Emperor Constantine The Great
He Studied Others To Become The Best Administrator Of The Ancient World

Inflation had left the Roman Empire in poverty. The denari had lost much of its value and was being counted in the thousands. There were charges of price gouging by "unbridled madmen." The army was at the mercy of "profiteers . . . who extorted prices not fourfold, not eightfold, but so great that human speech cannot describe."

In desperation Emperor Diocletian issued an edict in 301 A.D. setting price ceilings on hundreds of products, from beer to breastplates. He also limited wages for scores of vital occupations — carpenters, bakers, plasterers, stonecutters, teachers and teamsters.

The edict was a disaster. Shortages appeared as products moved to the black market. Corruption circumvented enforcement. In time, the government gave up. Years later, Emperor Constantine, who reigned from 306 to 337 A.D., remembered the failed edict and resolved not to repeat it.

Instead, he attacked the problem at its root. He knew that people had to be confident in their currency to keep the market stable. He issued a new gold coin he named the solidus, which means solid.

It was minted 72 to the pound and kept consistently pure. Constantine put hundreds of thousands of the new coins into circulation. This, he figured, would keep the solidus from being hoarded.

People became so confident the solidus was real money that the economy stabilized. The solidus remained in use for seven centuries as the dollar of medieval Europe.

Flavius Valerius Constantinus, or Constantine the Great (272–337 A.D.), was a revolutionary leader. After three decades of divided rule, he united the Roman Empire under one ruler.

He instituted broad reforms for a stable economy, religious freedom, humane treatment of people, secure borders and sound government. His reforms laid the foundations of the Byzantine Empire, which lasted more than 1,000 years.

Watch And Learn

How did he do it? By studying others' mistakes.

When Constantine was a young man, four emperors — led by Diocletian — ruled the Roman Empire. Constantine's father, Constantius Chlorus, was one of the four.

To ensure Chlorus' good behavior, Diocletian kept Constantine at his court in Nicomedia (modern Izmit, Turkey). There, Constantine watched politics up close to learn all he could.

Diocletian was a reformer with a strong sense of public service. After 20 years as emperor, he shocked the world by retiring, leaving his handpicked successors in charge.

Constantine absorbed his sense of duty from both Diocletian and his father. He also adopted Diocletian's interest in reform. But Diocletian had tried to hurry things. He was a soldier and expected to rule by command.

Constantine, on the other hand, understood the value of persuasion to get what he wanted. Good public relations, he knew, would help him sway the most people to his side.

Take his dealings with the Christians. He wasn't a Christian at Diocletian's court, but he saw firsthand how Diocletian's heavy-handed persecution of Christians burdened the court system and alienated many good citizens.

He was also impressed by the Christians' strong faith. He realized, too, that the Christians could potentially provide strong support for him as sole emperor.

He analyzed their traits. The Christians were organized, highly motivated and loyal to their protectors.

Constantine decided he needed their support. He actively pursued their favor. In his Edict of Milan in 313 A.D., he made religious freedom the empire's policy, allowing Christians and everyone else freedom to follow the religion each might desire.

When Constantine saw a policy he liked, he adapted it. For instance, he based much of his legislation on Christian morals. He banned crucifixion. He outlawed the separation of slave families and the killing of slaves by their owners. He made Sunday a day of rest.

His strategy worked — in the civil wars that followed, Christians gave Constantine their support.

But most citizens of the empire weren't Christians, and Constantine didn't want to alienate them. Although he embraced many Christian practices (and became a Christian on his deathbed), he didn't make Christianity the state religion.

"It was not just a cynical political calculation. Constantine saw that these Christians persevered in their faith," said Dimitrios Kousoulas, author of "The Life and Times of Constantine the Great." "He came to believe that he was the chosen instrument of God."

Gradual Change

When Constantine wanted something changed, he proceeded gradually. "This gradualness was one of his principal talents and virtues," wrote Michael Grant in "Constantine the Great."

For example, he despised the popular gladiatorial games. Yet he knew he couldn't outlaw them without sparking riots and maybe a revolt.

So he took the long-term approach. He barred judges from sentencing convicts to the arena. This dried up the supply of gladiators. The games withered and eventually disappeared.

Constantine saw that power struggles could crush an empire. While Diocletian had shared power to maintain control over the vast empire, his system fell apart quickly after he retired. Too many military commanders wanted to be emperors.

When Constantine emerged in 323 A.D. as sole emperor after years of civil war, he divided duties between military and civilian officials to thwart challengers. In 324 A.D., Constantine finally achieved full control over an undivided empire. He relocated the imperial headquarters to Byzantium, and he changed the name of the city to Constantinople. He also divided command of the army, appointing a master of infantry, a master of cavalry and a master of field forces.

To make sure he got the most up-to-date information, Constantine also established an independent corps of "agents of affairs," who regularly reported goings-on in the empire to him. This made it possible for him to allow deputies considerable autonomy without fear of losing control.

In fact, he allowed his most senior civil administrators so much freedom that he even refused to hear appeals of their decisions. As long as things went well, he didn't interfere. The system continued smoothly until his death in 337 A.D.

31

Aviator James H. Doolittle
Careful Preparation Helped
Turn The Tide In World War II

When Jimmy Doolittle readied his land-based bomber for take-off from the aircraft carrier USS Hornet on April 18, 1942, he felt the eyes of hundreds gazing at him — all the members of his mission and the carrier's crew.

While others might feel that the pressure cooker had been turned up, Army Air Forces Col. Doolittle stayed calm and focused.

"I felt completely comfortable and confident as our B-25 was placed in the takeoff position and the wheels chocked," Doolittle wrote in his autobiography "I Could Never Be So Lucky Again."

His confidence would prove prophetic. Doolittle's groundbreaking aviation strategies and tactics changed the way war is fought. The methods are still taught today.

When President Franklin D. Roosevelt and the military's top brass first floated the idea of an airstrike on Japan to retaliate for the Dec. 7, 1941, bombing of Pearl Harbor, their main concern had been how to launch big enough planes from an aircraft carrier. Carriers' runways were less than eight feet wider than the narrowest long-range bomber, the B-25.

Doolittle (1896–1993) knew that the members of his raiding party were all highly skilled, but they'd never taken off from a carrier before. Aware that preparation was the best teacher, Doolittle had his men learn and nearly overlearn the short takeoffs required to get the big planes aloft in a short space.

Even before that, Doolittle and his pilots noticed something else. When a carrier was moving, planes could lift off at lower speeds using less runway. Navy pilots already used this knowledge in launching their smaller, lighter planes. Taking a cue from the Navy, Army pilots incorporated the maneuver.

Doolittle's mission was much more involved than taking off, flying to Japan and dropping bombs. Planes had to be altered to carry more fuel and to sight targets at low altitudes. Targets in Japan had to be identified and routes and logistics planned.

He'd prepared for such a mission for years. He'd taken up flying at age 20, when he joined the Army in World War I. While he never saw combat, he knew pilots needed to be ready for anything. He kept that at the forefront of his mind when he taught others how to fly.

The more he flew, the more he believed that piloting was about "learning your limitations and staying within them — but constantly expanding your limitations."

The Army and Navy both had their own air corps in World War I. But outside of the armed forces, planes were little used. There was no commercial aviation then.

Fascinated by flight, Doolittle stayed in the Army after the war, mainly because the War Department had a budget to develop and promote new aircraft technology.

He jumped at every opportunity to try new air tactics. He flew test flights to determine operating limits of planes. He also took part in numerous air shows and races put on to demonstrate and promote the use of planes to the public.

To make better planes, the Army wanted pilots who were also engineers. Doolittle, who looked constantly for ways to improve, volunteered to go through its mechanics, parachute and engineering schools. Later, he became one of the first pilots to earn graduate degrees in aeronautical engineering from the Massachusetts Institute of Technology.

Doolittle made staying organized a priority. From engineering school instructor Col. Thurman Bane, Doolittle learned his lifelong habit of keeping a small personal notebook. At one end, Doolittle kept a chronology of things to do. At the other end, he kept an alphabetized set of notes for a permanent record.

Doolittle wanted to put his education to use "to help solve some problems that plagued aviation and threatened to stymie its growth."

At the same time, "being competitive by nature, I thoroughly enjoyed stunting, racing and trying to outdo my contemporaries in the air. Winning and excelling was always my goal."

He managed to combine adventure with science a number of times. Doolittle was the first person to safely execute a blind, or instrument-guided, flight in conditions of no visibility — in dense fog — in 1929.

To stretch his own skills, Doolittle looked for a situation that would let him test cutting-edge aircraft development. He found it with Shell Oil.

Shell executives were convinced that commercial flight would take hold and wanted to be ready to compete in the aviation fuel market. Doolittle left active duty in 1930 to join Shell. He tested Shell products and promoted its name in long-distance demonstration flights worldwide. The job brought him into contact with industry and government leaders everywhere.

Doolittle loved a challenge, and he tried to outdo himself every time he got into a cockpit. In 1932, he broke world speed records for flight.

Ever the patriot, he remained in the Army Reserves until going back on active duty in July 1940. Gen. Henry Arnold put Doolittle to work procuring planes from industry. Arnold then called on him to plot the air raid on Tokyo. Doolittle had just slightly more than two months to get the mission ready.

"I felt the need to straighten out in my mind what had been done and what needed to be done to get trained crews and combat-ready airplanes to the debarkation port by April 1," he said. "As I had done before and many times since, I closed my office door and wrote a memo to clarify my thinking and make sure I hadn't forgotten anything."

He laid out the details of the raid, from its purpose down to obtaining weather reports.

"It had been my experience in industry that plans that included new methods or devices and involved other people must always be followed up, because, as the saying goes, 'There's always someone who doesn't get the message,'" Doolittle wrote. "In this case, there would probably be people who didn't appreciate the urgency of what I wanted done, and I wouldn't be able to tell them the why of it all."

To make sure his strict standards were maintained, Doolittle insisted that he command the project. His superiors fought him.

Arnold didn't want him to be lost in a dangerous raid. But Doolittle lobbied and held his ground, and he prevailed in the end. The Tokyo raid was his first combat mission.

Crews of the 16 planes in the raid had all been through much the same drills. All were bound for Japan, and most of them for Tokyo. But once they left the Hornet, they were on their own. They used no radios so as to avoid detection by Japan.

Doolittle knew surprising an opponent gave the upper hand. His attack strategy relied on surprise.

One of the navigators, 1st Lt. James Macia, explained how this worked: "Each airplane was operating independently of the others. After a 700-mile flight over water with no navigation aids except a compass, the aircraft had drifted off course by as much as 15 miles right or left. As a result, planes were approaching their targets from every direction and at varying intervals. This caused great confusion and gave the impression that there were many more than 16 attacking planes."

The raid succeeded in confusing and scaring the Japanese. Although the planes were all lost when the pilots ran out of fuel and had to crash-land in China, the raid itself was a great shot in the arm for U.S. morale, which had sunk with Pearl Harbor and defeats in the Pacific.

Doolittle wasn't about to sit back and live off the kudos the raid engendered. Promoted to general, he went on to command the 12th Army Air Forces during the North Africa campaign in 1942–43, the 15th Army Air Forces in Italy in 1943 and the 8th Army Air Forces during the bombing offensive against Germany in 1944–45.

32

Indian Emperor Akbar The Great

Rethinking Old Ways Strengthened His Rule

When Abu-ul-Fath Jalal-ud-Din Muhammad Akbar, a Muslim, ascended the throne in India at age 13 in the 16th century, the Mughal Empire was on the verge of collapse.

Muslims had conquered India during the prior 500 years. Akbar (1542–1605), better known to history as Akbar the Great, was a descendant of the Mongol invader Tamerlane and Genghis Khan.

The Mughal dynasty founded by Akbar's grandfather 30 years earlier had controlled northern India, but Akbar's father had barely been able to hang on to the Punjab region and the area around the city of Delhi.

There was only one way, as Akbar saw it, to reassert his authority: war. Though he was but a youth, Akbar began fighting his way across the subcontinent and rebuilding the empire.

As the years went by, however, he recognized the need for diplomacy. He saw one sure-fire way to ensure the peaceful cooperation of Hindu princes in the area — marriage. He agreed to marry a Hindu princess to solidify an alliance.

He discovered that Hindus weren't the evil people he'd thought. His exposure to his wife's religion and culture helped him vanquish his prejudices. Thinking about his own reaction, he began to see that if he could induce others to be equally tolerant, he could create a stable empire.

Instead of oppressing non-Muslims, he made them equal to Muslims in the eyes of the law and ended special taxes they had to pay. He discouraged the slaughter of cows out of respect for Hindu beliefs and participated in Hindu religious festivals. He granted freedom of religion and allowed Christian missionary work.

Although illiterate — historians believe he might've suffered from dyslexia — he had a powerful mind, and he wanted to learn. He had books read to him, both sacred and secular. He commissioned translations of Sanskrit texts into the Persian language of the court so others could learn as well.

To encourage new ideas, he built a special "house of worship," where yogis, Muslims of various sects, Jesuits, Zoroastrian priests and others could discuss religion with Akbar and each other. This wasn't an age of easy tolerance: Some Muslim clerics were highly upset with his open-minded approach. "Akbar walked warily but steadily," wrote Ishtiaq Hussain Qureshi in his book "Akbar."

All this was in stark contrast with Europe, which was in the midst of the Inquisition and of wars and persecution during the Reformation.

"He was the first powerful Muslim ruler in India who seriously attempted to bring Muslims and Hindus together," wrote Kamal Srivastava in "Two Great Mughals." "He certainly helped them to coexist with each other."

Akbar decided to help foster this spirit and create a sense of national unity by developing a new Mughal culture that transcended a particular religion. He funded artistic projects that blended Hindu and Muslim styles to encourage the idea that the two religions could exist together. (The most famous result was the Taj Mahal, built by his grandson.)

Akbar realized that more than treating everyone equally regardless of religion was needed to create a strong and just society. He decreed that the justice system must treat rich and poor alike. He outlawed slavery, infanticide and child marriages.

He changed the way land revenues were assessed to ease the burden on peasants. The traditional demand for a third of gross produce from all farmers was replaced by fair cash payments calculated after an assessment of local yields and prices. Agriculture subsequently flourished during his reign, and European visitors wrote with wonder about the lushness of the Mughal realm.

Akbar's most enduring impact on India was his reorganization of the way it was administered. The British viceroys modeled their system on his and passed this on to India, Pakistan and Bangladesh.

"Previous Indian governments had been weakened by the tendency of armies to split up into the private forces of individual commanders and the tendency of provincial governors to become hereditary local rulers," said Kenneth Ballhatchet, professor of the history of South Asia at the University of London.

Akbar battled this tendency with several reforms. He centralized the civil service and the military, bringing them both under his direct command. The changes made it easier for Akbar to keep tabs on events and opened career opportunities for the most able and ambitious administrators to move between the two types of government employment.

Unlike previous Indian rulers, Akbar didn't pay attention to religion or ethnic background when he spotted people with administrative or military skill.

To streamline information and finances, Akbar set up a centralized financial system with revenue collectors working alongside each provincial governor, but reporting only to the emperor. A network of official correspondents provided him with news from across his far-flung empire, which he expanded to include northern and central India as well as what is today Afghanistan, Pakistan and Bangladesh.

The Mughal government received annual income equivalent to 32 million English pounds at a time when Queen Elizabeth I in her last five years could count on less than a half-million pounds annually, Srivastava says.

"It was the most splendorous empire of his age, and Akbar's fame traveled far and wide into every corner of the then-known world," Qureshi said. "Little wonder that he has passed into the folklore of his former empire as a just and benevolent monarch."

33

Military Strategist Karl von Clausewitz

His 10-Volume Battle Plan Elevated This General To The Rank Of Expert

When it came to war, Karl von Clausewitz said the only thing certain was uncertainty.

A professional soldier who first saw combat at 13, Clausewitz (1780–1831) went on to achieve the rank of general in the Prussian army and the status of legend for his 10 volumes on warfare. The most notable of these were his three volumes titled "On War," considered by many experts to be the most important and influential work ever written on the subject. Studied in military colleges the world over, his writings have influenced many, including U.S. generals Dwight Eisenhower and George Patton.

In war, Clausewitz wrote, a battle plan must be by necessity everchanging, for good reason.

"Earlier theorists aimed to equip the conduct of war with principles, rules or even systems, and thus considered only factors that could be mathematically calculated (e.g., numerical superiority, supply, the base, interior lines). All these attempts are objectionable, however, because they aim at fixed values. In war everything is uncertain and variable, intertwined with psychological forces and effects, and the product of a continuous interaction of opposites," wrote Clausewitz in "On War."

"Clausewitz's fundamental basic point is that warfare isn't simple. It is an inherently complex, dynamic, changing environment, and you have to be conscious of that. You're not a craftsman out there doing the same thing over and over again," said Christopher Bassford, a Clausewitz expert who teaches at the National War College in Washington, D.C.

Many of the strategic, philosophical and leadership principles of "On War" have been embraced and adapted by the business community.

"Clausewitz summed up what it had all been about in his classic 'On War,'" wrote former General Electric Chairman and Chief Executive Jack Welch. "Men could not reduce strategy to a formula. Instead, the human elements were paramount: leadership, morale and the almost instinctive savvy of the best generals."

Clausewitz and the Prussian general staff, Welch wrote, "did not expect a plan of operations to survive beyond the first contact with the enemy. They set only the broadest of objectives and emphasized seizing unforeseen opportunities as they arose. Strategy was not a lengthy action plan. It was the evolution of a central idea through continually changing circumstances."

Clausewitz the soldier demonstrated his bravery in many instances on the battlefield. "Courage, above all things, is the first quality of a warrior," he said, adding that if not present naturally, it could emerge as a result of proper training.

Clausewitz was known for his sterling reputation, personal integrity and honesty. Because his works — in his time and now — were considered to be difficult reads, many of his famous quotes have been taken out of context and have created "the popular misconception of Clausewitz as a cold and callous prophet of total, unconditional war. . . . Yet it is precisely Clausewitz's train of logic that merits the full attention of those interested in strategic thinking and practice," wrote Tiha von Ghyczy, Bolko von Oetinger and Christopher Bassford in "Clausewitz on Strategy: Inspiration and Insight from a Master Strategist."

Eye On Tomorrow

Clausewitz thoroughly studied his own ideas and those of others. He wasn't writing for fame, recognition or money, but only to help future officers. He insisted that his wife, Marie, publish his major works — including "On War" — only after his death so they would be free of speculation about his agenda.

"Clausewitz has a tremendous amount of intellectual integrity. He's interested in the truth and doesn't care where it goes. Clausewitz is honest," Bassford said.

That honesty struck a chord with Clausewitz's contemporary, the Duke of Wellington, Bassford said. Wellington, who defeated Napoleon at Waterloo with the help of England's German allies, wrote a 25-page memo about only one analysis of the battle — Clausewitz's.

Clausewitz played an important role at Waterloo as chief of staff to Gen. J.A. von Thielmann, head of Prussia's 3rd Army Corps.

Decisiveness in battle was necessary for victory, Clausewitz wrote: "It is even better to act quickly and err than to hesitate until the time of action is past." He said great leaders have audacity and should take calculated risks.

"In what field of human activity is boldness more at home than in war?" he wrote. "It must be granted a certain power over and above successful calculations involving space, time and magnitude of forces."

Flexibility, Clausewitz believed, was key in the chaos of battle. "Presence of mind is nothing but an increased capacity of dealing with the unexpected," he wrote. Military genius wasn't a God-given gift but could be developed: "It is the inquiring rather than the creative mind, the comprehensive rather than the specialized approach, the calm rather than the excitable head" that won battles.

While Clausewitz was a professional soldier, he didn't limit his thinking to military matters. His interest in and studies of art, science, education, history and political theory gave depth to his writings on war. "It was his refusal, above everything else, to let his mind be constrained to a narrow point of view that must strike the modern professional as exemplary," wrote Ghyczy, Oetinger and Bassford.

Man Of Principle

His ability to look at the big picture helped him solve immediate problems, too. After France and Napoleon defeated Prussia in 1806, Prussian King Frederick Wilhelm III conscripted troops to fight for France against Russia in order to avoid his country's destruction. Clausewitz, along with other officers, stuck to their principles and resigned their commissions rather than fight with Napoleon.

Clausewitz believed that if the Russians beat Napoleon, he could liberate his fellow Prussians. So he and other officers joined the Russian army to help that happen.

Once the Russian army repelled Napoleon's attack on Moscow, Clausewitz took action in 1812. He crossed lines in disguise, and encouraged the Prussian commander and others to join him with the Russians. They did, which led to a treaty with Russia and forced the Prussian king to break with Napoleon.

"Clausewitz as a man is as worthy as the work ('On War') itself," wrote Ghyczy, Oetinger and Bassford. "His values and intrinsic beliefs, more than his specific ideas, have given his work an inner coherence and a power of persuasion that have endured until modern days. He may rightly be seen as an inspiration to all those whose ambition is to excel professionally in any field."

34

Rear Adm.
Grace Murray Hopper
Her Determination Helped
Computerize Defense

Grace Murray Hopper wasn't about to let anyone tell her what she could do.

It was the middle of World War II, and Hopper was working for the U.S. Navy. She'd been assigned to use a new computer to find precise aiming angles for guns in varying weather conditions. But her peers thought Hopper was crazy. Why did a woman think she could solve computer problems no one else could?

Shrugging off the jeers she heard each day, Hopper (1906–92) focused all her energy on the problem.

Assigned to the Bureau of Ordnance Computation at Harvard University, Hopper was told to use the Mark I computer — which no one had mastered — to find the angles.

Where others saw defeat, Hopper saw challenge. She fell in love with the 51-foot-long, 8-foot-high, 8-foot-wide, glass-encased hunk of relays, switches and vacuum tubes.

She spent countless hours inputting codes, figuring out what the computer could do. She logged everything she did so she could retrace her steps after a mistake. She became the Mark I's first programmer.

Finally, her work paid off. Thanks to her coding, the computer spit out the correct aiming angles.

Hopper's innovative ideas included software development concepts, data processing and computer verification. She wasn't afraid of change. Her early recognition of the potential of computers spearheaded the way for modern data processing and sparked the computerization of defense systems.

Love For Learning

Born in New York City, Grace Brewster Murray was the oldest of three children. From a very young age, she was very curious and liked to disassemble household gadgets to see how they worked.

Hopper's early family influence taught her to reach beyond typical feminine roles. As a girl, she got high marks in school and was accustomed to being at the head of her class.

By 1928, she'd graduated Phi Beta Kappa from Vassar College with a bachelor's in mathematics and physics. In 1930, she received a master's in mathematics and physics, and in 1934 she received a Ph.D. in mathematics from Yale University. That same year, she married Vincent Hopper, an English instructor at New York University.

In 1931, Hopper began teaching math for $800 per year at Vassar. To grab students' attention, she used examples of the role math played in real life. In a probability course, she had the students play bridge and dice games. In another course, Hopper had the students plan a city and figure out how to finance it.

Hopper was promoted to associate professor, but with the outbreak of World War II, she wanted to do more to serve her country. After her husband died during World War II, Hopper tried to join the Navy herself.

At 34 years old and just 105 pounds, Navy officials insisted that Hopper was overage and underweight. They told her that she was more valuable as a mathematics professor.

Hopper had prepared herself for their arguments. She produced a waiver for her weight requirement, special permission from the government and a leave of absence from Vassar.

She was sworn into the U.S. Naval Reserve in December 1943, and she graduated first in her class at Midshipman's School for Women.

After the war, Hopper looked for more challenges. She joined the Eckert-Mauchly Computer Corp. in Philadelphia, later called

Sperry Rand, in 1949, to design a computer even faster than the Mark I. The UNIVAC I would be the first commercial large-scale electronic digital computer.

Hopper wanted to make the computer both programmer-friendly and application-friendly. She spent countless hours transcribing and hand-copying codes for a shared library of programs. As a result, she reduced computing errors, tedium and duplication of effort.

In 1949, Hopper and her team developed the first compiler, the A-O. This computer translated mathematical codes into machine codes and stored them on magnetic tape. This development enabled operators to find data faster than ever before.

Bigger And Better

Now Hopper expanded her vision. She was convinced that computers could be more user-friendly — and that they could understand a programming language using English words.

Colleagues told her it was impossible. Hopper dug in harder, determined to make her vision a reality.

She began work on the B-O compiler, later known as the FLOW-MATIC. By equating numbers with the English alphabet, she taught the computer to recognize 20 statements in English.

If one computer could do it, so could they all, Hopper reasoned. She began a campaign to persuade her peers to develop a new common business computer language. The result was COBOL — Common-Business-Oriented Language.

To help sell everyone on COBOL, Hopper met with business managers to explain the feasibility of the English language compilers. She participated in public demonstrations by the Sperry Corporation and RCA.

Her public demonstrations and private lobbying persuaded the entire Navy to use the computer language. Soon other branches of the service adopted it as well.

Hopper's work changed other programming languages. It eventually led to the international standards for most programming languages.

While totally focused on her work, Hopper strived to keep the atmosphere around her lighthearted. Known among her co-workers as "Amazing Grace," she laughingly referred to herself as "the little old lady who talks to computers." She set the clock in her office to run backward, and she had a flag on her wall with a skull and crossbones.

Hopper looked for precise ways to express herself, and if a word didn't exist to describe a new experience, she'd make one up that did. Take her coining of the term "bug." Once when tracing an error in the Mark II, she found a moth trapped in a relay. The bug was carefully removed and taped into a logbook. She and her team referred to the "bug" whenever a computer had a problem.

In 1969, Hopper received the first ever Computer Science Man-of-the-Year Award from the Data Processing Management Association. In 1971, the Sperry Corporation initiated an annual award in her name to honor young computer professionals for their significant contributions to computer science. In 1973, she became the first person from the U.S. and the first woman of any nationality to be made a Distinguished Fellow of the British Computer Society. Elevated to rear admiral in November 1985, she was one of a few women admirals in the history of the Navy.

Hopper refused to slow down even in retirement. Once she quit the Navy in 1986, she immediately took a job as a senior consultant to Digital Equipment Corporation. She remained there several years, working well into her 80s. She often spoke at engineering forums, colleges, universities and computer seminars. Hopper died Jan. 1, 1992.

35

OSS Founder
William Donovan
His Careful Study Helped
U.S. Gain Intelligence Lead

Williamm "Wild Bill" Donovan spent his honeymoon spying for the U.S.

The 1919 mission — he interrupted an idyll in Japan to see how the Russian Revolution was winding down in Siberia — wouldn't go unnoticed. Later, during World War II, he was tapped to form America's first serious intelligence agency, the Office of Strategic Services (OSS).

Donovan, a Columbia University classmate of Franklin D. Roosevelt, was a natural to be at the top of President FDR's short list of candidates.

A World War I Medal of Honor recipient, Donovan (1883–1959) continued to devour news from abroad after his military service. He also scoured history books for lessons to be applied in a future conflict many Americans at the time didn't think possible.

"He was quite a great reader," said Elizabeth McIntosh, a White House correspondent who joined the OSS and then served in the field in Burma and India. "He based OSS guerrilla tactics in World War II on those used by Mosby's Raiders in the Civil War."

As a prominent western New York lawyer, Donovan networked with other leading figures to share his thoughts and emerge as a leader who knew world affairs.

So when the time came to staff the OSS, "Donovan practically turned his address book inside out, and people came flocking," said OSS veteran S. Peter Karlow, author of the first history of the OSS.

Donovan's dogged persistence helped defeat Nazi Germany and Japan, historians concur. His legacy likely helped the U.S. win the Cold War, and continues today to aid U.S. efforts.

Information Clearinghouse

While most Americans saw fascists in Europe and militarists in Japan as unlikely threats, FDR and Donovan feared the worst. Democrat FDR disagreed with Republican Donovan on most issues, but both believed the U.S. was unprepared for a looming world war.

Right up to Pearl Harbor, several federal agencies made up a loosely knit intelligence operation. No central authority gathered and assessed information.

FDR changed that. He turned first to Donovan, who had traveled widely in the 1930s studying the changing world on his own and for the government.

In Ethiopia, Donovan saw firsthand Italy's military in the field. He also attended German army maneuvers. Back home, he gave detailed reports to the White House. His most important assignment: a 1939 tour of England. There he experienced the Luftwaffe's airstrikes on Britain.

He came home convinced the U.S. would soon be at war and needed Britain as an ally. So he threw his law firm into action, researching the legal brief for FDR's lend-lease program, which sent U.S. warships to Britain in exchange for setting up U.S. naval and air bases on British soil.

The OSS wasn't chartered until mid-1942. Its real birthday: Dec. 7, 1941, the day Japan attacked Pearl Harbor. That's when Donovan's warning became clear: The U.S. needed to know what other powers had planned for it — or suffer for its ignorance.

"That goal wouldn't be fully met during World War II, but Donovan led policy-makers to accept its necessity," noted Abram N. Shelsky, author of "Silent Warfare: Understanding the World of Intelligence."

Donovan convinced policy-makers by setting up the OSS. He created a service that would compensate for years of inattention.

How? By gathering plentiful information so policy-makers could make good decisions.

"It was a paradigm shift for the U.S.," said Ken deGraffenreid, a professor at Boston University's Institute for World Politics. "Donovan clearly got U.S. intelligence into a modern mode of thinking."

He viewed intelligence work as an essential and constant duty. He wanted people adept at gathering, analyzing, and reporting information, so he turned to universities to staff the OSS.

He wasn't bogged down by social conventions. Women made up a quarter of the OSS staff, playing a big role producing much-needed reports.

In "War: Ends and Means," intelligence scholars Paul Seabury and Angelo Codevilla note how Donovan had the OSS match personnel to its paramilitary and espionage missions — and how it paid off.

"It sent leftists to leftists and rightists to rightists," they wrote. "As a result, disparate elements were enlisted to fight on the American side."

Historian Thomas Troy points out that Donovan had a single goal in mind: winning the war.

Donovan wouldn't close the door on options. He once told an aide, "I'd put Stalin on the OSS payroll if I thought it would help us defeat Hitler."

Donovan sometimes faced hostility. Gen. Douglas MacArthur kept the OSS out of his Southwest Pacific theater. FBI Director J. Edgar Hoover kept the OSS out of Latin America.

Donovan didn't dwell on the snubs — at least not in public. Instead, he sought opportunities close to where the OSS had been shut out. Small OSS fighting units sent into Burma and China, countries outside MacArthur's domain, tied down much larger Japanese forces.

Europe was another matter. Gen. Dwight D. Eisenhower appreciated how OSS agents coaxed Vichy officials in North Africa not to resist American troop landings. That coup led to the Allies' driving Axis forces there back to Italy. Ike even had the OSS organize and supply the French resistance before the Normandy invasion. OSS activity saved the lives of an estimated 10,000 Allied troops in southern France alone. OSS agents helped Allied planners by brokering the surrender of German forces on the Italian front.

The OSS succeeded over and over, but it failed enough that it gave its rivals in government an opening. When FDR died, Donovan lost his patron. President Harry S. Truman, who disliked Donovan, disbanded the OSS in 1945.

But in 1947, Truman launched the Central Intelligence Agency. Donovan wouldn't be its head, but his influence was still obvious. Veterans of the OSS would be the CIA's cadre. CIA directors Allen Dulles, William Colby, Richard Helms and William Casey were OSS veterans.

The CIA still echoes the OSS. There's the cloak-and-dagger branch, but there's also the CIA's less-publicized analysis branch, just as Donovan — having learned how unpreparedness led to World War II — planned it.

36

Military Strategist
John Boyd

His Bold Tactics Changed
The Way We Fight — And Win

The Pentagon didn't officially thank the late Air Force Col. John Boyd for his contributions to the U.S. military's rout of Saddam Hussein's forces in 2003. But in the Officers Club at Fort Meyer, not far from Washington, D.C., a group of regulars raised a toast to praise what Boyd meant to the victory.

To members of this group, which has gathered each Wednesday night the past two decades, Boyd's revolutionary ideas about warfare are tied to the victory in Iraq.

Boyd's biographer Robert Coram calls Boyd "one of the most important unknown men of his time. He did what so few men are privileged to do: He changed the world."

Boyd (1927–97) was one of the most accomplished fighter pilots of his generation. He literally wrote the book on the aerial warfare techniques used today by U.S. pilots.

Just as important, Boyd was a top engineer and project leader in the development of the F-16, now the most widely used fighter jet in the world. And he is the architect of a combat theory, known as the "OODA Loop," that many, including Vice President Dick Cheney, have credited for transforming the U.S. military. The loop theory is thought to have helped the U.S. win the 1991 Gulf War and prevail in Operation Iraqi Freedom.

Coram put it simply: "Boyd is the most influential military thinker since Sun Tzu wrote 'The Art of War' 2,400 years ago."

Eye On His Goal

Growing up humbly in Erie, Pa., Boyd was fascinated by airplanes. He spent his teen-age years working three jobs to help support his mother and four siblings after their father died. But his goal was to fly. So as soon as he could, at the age of 18, he joined the Army Air Forces.

The Army, though, wouldn't let Boyd in the cockpit. Temporarily changing his focus, he left the Army two years after he enlisted to get an economics degree. But he didn't give up on his goal.

Instead, Boyd joined the Air Force ROTC at the University of Iowa, and he received his commission as an officer when he graduated in 1951.

It didn't take long for Boyd to prove the Army wrong for grounding him. He flew nearly three dozen combat missions in the Korean War.

When the fighting ended, Boyd decided to share the firsthand knowledge he'd picked up in the air by becoming a flight instructor. He soon earned the nickname "40-second Boyd" for a challenge he laid down to all his trainees: If he couldn't beat them in a dogfight within 40 seconds, he'd pay them $40.

Boyd never had to pay.

When he wasn't flying, Boyd was learning. He devoured books on calculus and engineering to try and pick up techniques that would make him a better pilot and trainer.

Gen. Charles Krulak, the former commandant of the Marine Corps, once said Boyd had an "unrelenting love of study."

"He was the quintessential soldier-scholar," Krulak said.

Boyd's learning paid off for the Air Force, too. By the Vietnam era, he'd written the "Aerial Attack Study." It details attack maneuvers and the physics behind them. It was the first real study of the strategy of air combat. And it's become required reading for all U.S. fighter pilots.

Passion For Perfection

Boyd's thirst for knowledge and tireless work ethic didn't stop with fighter planes. He was driven to innovate, so much so that he upset many of his superiors in the military, particularly those who feared to change the Pentagon's status quo.

Boyd believed the Pentagon's top brass were too concerned with buying big, flashy, expensive weapon systems. He thought they weren't concerned enough about creating systems that worked well and were adaptable to changing combat situations.

In one display of his passion for perfection, Boyd got into a shouting match with an official from a defense contractor in a Pentagon cafeteria. Boyd repeatedly jabbed a lit cigar in the official's chest, burning a hole in the man's tie.

Such outbursts came at a cost. Boyd narrowly avoided two different court-martial proceedings. But he was more concerned about improvements in the military than the advancement of his own rank, Coram says.

Determined to make the improvements, Boyd left the Air Force in 1975, even though he might've been on track to become a general. He spent the rest of his life working as a private military contractor.

"My goal was not personal," Boyd once said. "My work was for the best interest of the country. I tried to do it the Air Force way and was refused at every turn. Then I did it my way."

In the end, Boyd's work, among other things, produced the "energy maneuverability theory." That idea is the core engineering concept behind the development of today's top fighter jets. It was also a breakthrough that helped Boyd and a team of followers design the F-16. That fighter is the world's leader, used by 22 countries.

While Boyd ruffled some military feathers, he won many fans. Plain spoken, blunt and sometimes even crass, Boyd was nonetheless an effective communicator.

Throughout his career, Boyd developed an extensive network of knowledgeable employees and colleagues. Many people gravitated toward Boyd because he trusted them to make their own decisions and they trusted his integrity.

As Boyd once said, "People fight wars, not machines. And they use their minds."

Today those people meet in the Fort Meyer Officers Club to talk about Boyd and ways to better the armed forces.

Some have been instrumental in changing the way the Pentagon develops and tests weapon systems.

Boyd's greatest legacy may be the "OODA Loop." It stands for "observe, orient, decide, act."

"Boyd," Coram said, "borrowing from Sun Tzu, said the best commander is one who wins while avoiding battle. The intent is to shatter cohesion, produce paralysis and bring about the collapse of the adversary by generating confusion, disorder, panic and chaos."

It was just that kind of strategy that was used in both wars against Iraq. And Boyd developed it only after extensive study.

Already a self-taught expert in air combat and engineering, Boyd read the works of every known military philosopher and studied tactics used in hundreds of battles. Then he found the common patterns that linked the winners of those battles.

PART 5

Taking Risks Creates Opportunity

©Bettmann/CORBIS

Take a method and try it. If it fails, admit it frankly
and try another. But above all, try something.

— FRANKLIN D. ROOSEVELT

37

Activist Lech Walesa

His Resolve To Change
The System Without Violence
Helped Free Poland

Organizing workers, Lech Walesa learned, wasn't as easy as it looked. If not done properly, it could have tragic consequences.

It was December 1970. Poland's communist government had doubled food and fuel prices without offering parallel wage increases. Poles everywhere went on strike.

Walesa, then 27, worked in Gdansk near the Baltic Sea at the Lenin Shipyard, where he belonged to the strike committee. He led 3,000 workers to a nearby police building. They demanded the firing of Polish Communist Party leader Wladyslaw Gomulka and threw stones at the building, set it ablaze and beat up employees trying to escape.

Soon, the crowd swelled to 10,000 angry workers, and Walesa called for calm. But it was too late; the crowd, out of control, continued to riot. Police retaliated with gunfire. Dozens of people died, and at least 300 were injured.

Although Walesa tried to quell the uprising, he knew he was to blame for inciting it. He vowed to organize only peaceful demonstrations in the future.

"It was enough to be there, to hear the shots, to clear away the corpses, to watch the terrible burials by night," he said in Mary

Craig's book "Lech Walesa and His Poland." "It was enough to make a man remember for the rest of his life."

Redemption

Walesa saw a chance to redeem himself in August 1980, when the government again raised food prices. He'd been fired from the shipyard a few months earlier, but he sneaked into the area to help the workers stand up for their rights.

Walesa took charge and became the head of an interfactory strike committee. The committee eventually became the bargaining representative for some 500,000 strikers, who stretched from the Baltic to the coal-mining heartland of Silesia.

This time, he made sure there was no violence. When calling for a strike, he stressed the importance of orderly protests to the 6,000 workers. He banned alcoholic beverages during marches to prevent rowdiness.

Shipyard officials acquiesced. They granted workers a wage increase and restored Walesa to his former job. But smaller groups of Polish workers without any power still struggled.

Walesa didn't like that. He wanted fairness for all.

So he instructed shipyard employees to go back on strike unless workers across Poland received the same basic benefits. Workers throughout the country began calling for higher wages, better working conditions, free speech and free trade unions. Walesa soon galvanized about 10 million people into one labor union: Solidarity.

Led by Walesa, the committee launched a bold set of political demands — including the right to strike and to form free unions — that were unheard of in communist countries. At first, authorities refused even to discuss them. The demands were known as the "21 Postulates."

How did he persuade so many people to unite? He traveled from town to town, speaking to crowds about the need for a free society. So that they knew he understood the problems they faced, he told them, "We eat the same bread." When scolded for wearing dumpy, baggy clothes, he often said, "I'm a worker, and I will dress like one."

According to a Polish journalist, "(Walesa) could work a crowd like an actor onstage, never reading a speech — not even when addressing the pope — and never speaking too long, stabbing the air with an oversized hand, making all the right gestures with almost flawless timing. His real strength as a speaker was an ability to reduce complex issues to simple words and images that everyone could understand."

When negotiating with Polish officials, Walesa was tactful. He laid out union requests and stressed that he wanted reform, not destruction, of the government. He said he envisioned a country with a new sense of patriotism, peace, responsibility, sense and order.

He told Solidarity members to act the same way. He warned that their demands wouldn't be met if they became too pushy and that they would experience more hardships if strikes weren't used wisely and sparingly.

He insisted on strict discipline.

Walesa led Solidarity to a dramatic victory in late September 1980. He persuaded the government to meet all of the union's demands, and six Communist Party officials were fired. "Because of his refusal to let Solidarity resort to physical force, Lech Walesa is in the tradition of (Mohandas) Gandhi and Martin Luther King, an apostle of nonviolence," Craig said. Soon after, communist officials felt that Solidarity leaders like Walesa were gaining too much power. He was arrested in December 1981 and jailed for 11 months. The government outlawed Solidarity.

Free At Last

Even so, Walesa kept Solidarity alive underground, and the organization remained a symbol of freedom, pride and hope for Polish citizens. He received the Nobel Peace Prize in 1983. The ban ended in 1988 after another shipyard strike that year. In 1989, the communists allowed free elections for a new parliament in Poland. In 1990, Walesa became the country's first president chosen in free balloting in more than half a century. He served until 1995.

"In standing up to a government backed by the Soviet superpower, which did not allow dissenting points of view, Walesa faced a nearly impossible situation," Nathan Aaseng wrote in "The Peace Seekers: The Nobel Peace Prize." "But there was something about his forcefulness and confidence that brought the Polish people streaming to his side."

Communism and his resistance to it shaped much of Walesa's life. Born in 1943 in Popowo, a small village in eastern Poland, he was raised by his mother. His father, enslaved in a Nazi labor camp in World War II, died shortly after the war. Walesa came to sympathize with oppressed people.

At the time, Poland had just been incorporated into the Soviet Union's communist bloc in Eastern Europe. In Walesa's grade school, students were taught about Marxism and Leninism. Teachers often praised Soviet leader Josef Stalin, whose image was painted on school walls.

Most students believed the propaganda, but Walesa learned from talking with older family members that much of what he was told in school was a lie.

"If I could see very well that something or other was white, no one was going to persuade me that it was black," he said.

Walesa often argued with teachers who tried to force-feed students about communism. The school's headmaster once smashed a cane over his head.

Meanwhile, Walesa's mother, Feliksa, taught him about Polish history, and his patriotism grew. She read aloud from Polish classics, including the epic works of Polish novelist Henryk Sienkiewicz. Sienkiewicz described Polish society in the 1600s during wars against the Cossacks, Turks and Swedes. He praised the chivalry of the Polish knights. Walesa absorbed everything.

All of his mother's stories had the same moral. "They taught one to be honest, to strive always to better oneself, to be just and to call white, white and black, black," Walesa said.

In 1959, Walesa entered a trade school in Lipno, a small town near Popowo. He studied agricultural mechanization and received his certificate in 1961.

At the school, Walesa earned a reputation for leadership and organization. In his dormitory, students were sometimes responsible for sweeping the corridors. Walesa took the initiative to make sure it got done. He awakened other students at 6 a.m., assigning some to wash the floor and others to shine it. By the time the teachers were up, the floor looked immaculate.

"He was determined," one teacher said. "If he set his mind on doing something, he would do it."

When he began work as an electrician at the Lenin Shipyard in 1967, Walesa immediately approached his fellow workers and built friendships with many of them. He gained their trust, and they chose him to be a work inspector.

He then was free to talk to anyone at the plant about work-related issues. He learned of many workers' concerns. Some were alarming.

"In the shipyard, I could feel I was myself at last," he said. "I began to understand that inside me was a deep, irresistible urge to go out and change things."

Walesa lost his re-election campaign in 1995 to Alexander Kwasniewski, the head of the Democratic Left Alliance. He tried running again for president in 2000, but received less than 1% of the vote. Walesa still remains active in Polish politics, although he holds no government office.

The "21 Postulates" that hung on the Gdansk shipyards during the strike in 1980 are now registered as historic documents in the United Nations Educational, Scientific and Cultural Organization's "memory of the world" catalogue. The boards with their list are reportedly still hanging from the gates.

38

President
Franklin D. Roosevelt

His Straightforward Approach
Lifted America From Fear

Franklin Delano Roosevelt refused to succumb to the conventional wisdom.

In 1921, he contracted polio. As Alan Axelrod wrote in "Nothing to Fear: Lessons in Leadership From FDR," it was a life-threatening disease. It "paralyzed him, subjected him to a life of relentless pain and nearly ended his career in public service."

Everyone told him to retire. No one would vote for a handicapped politician. Roosevelt refused to listen.

Instead, he analyzed his situation. "He chose instead to understand polio, to see clearly the extent of his disability, and then to assess — also clearly — his options for overcoming his disability," said Axelrod. "He did not blink at the odds."

It was an attitude that helped make him one of our greatest presidents.

This wasn't the first time FDR battled the tide. Just the year before, he'd been the vice presidential candidate on a ticket headed by Ohio Gov. James Cox. Roosevelt knew that in the post–World War I isolationist atmosphere, he could never win, especially against Warren Harding's seductive promise of a "return to normalcy."

Still, Axelrod wrote, he remained positive. "Roosevelt did not take a defeatist attitude, and he did not conduct a perfunctory campaign.

Instead he regarded the run as a valuable opportunity to gain exposure, to express his ideas and to hone his campaign skills."

Roosevelt (1882–1945) was right. He remained active in politics, and in 1928 he won the first of two straight two-year terms as governor of New York. Four straight successful runs for president — the most ever — followed that. He died soon into his last term.

Crisis Management

Roosevelt became president in 1933, amid a difficult period in the nation's history. In the cities, jobs were being lost to the Great Depression. America's farmers were in an equally precarious position, hit by lower prices for produce on the one hand and the Dust Bowl on the other. The country was in disarray. Banks were failing, and there was widespread panic.

As he had shown in the 1932 campaign, Roosevelt wasn't a slave to what he called "absurd tradition." At the time, candidates didn't attend their parties' conventions to accept the nomination. In fact, they weren't even supposed to acknowledge the nomination for weeks, a tradition harking to the early days of the Republic when communications were slower.

FDR accepted the nomination in person because "these are unprecedented and unusual times. May this be a symbol of my intention to be obvious and to avoid all hypocrisy and sham."

Once elected, he recognized the first thing he had to do was be positive, to instill confidence in the nation. "The only thing we have to fear is fear itself," he told the nation in his inaugural address.

He set priorities. "I favor, as a practical policy, the putting of first things first," he said. International trade and relations would have to wait. "The emergency at home cannot wait."

He took quick action, too. In his first 100 days in office, he declared a bank holiday (to prevent a run on the banks), called Congress into emergency session and created a number of important new relief agencies. These included the Civilian Conservation Corps, the Civil Works Administration and the Public Works Administration. The CCC eventually employed 2.5 million people.

As the nation had never faced a crisis like this before, he didn't know whether his plan would work. But taking action was better than doing nothing. Roosevelt said in a *Time* magazine article that his technique of governing was "bold, persistent experimentation. Take a method and try it. If it fails, admit it frankly and try another. But above all, try something."

The First Great Communicator

To reach the greatest number of people, Roosevelt began using the new medium of radio for speeches while governor. It was a practice he continued as president with his regular fireside chats.

In these chats, he kept his message simple and his language inclusive. "We're all in this together," he said. "We must share together the bad news and the good news, the defeats and the victories."

His words were also chosen to inspire. He tried to make participation in the country's recovery seem more of a mission than an obligation. "To some generations, much is given. Of other generations much is expected," he said in a speech following his second nomination. "This generation has a rendezvous with destiny."

He recognized the importance of leading by example. Despite his illness, despite the difficulty of traveling at the time, he went to see the Dust Bowl crisis in person because he understood, as Axelrod wrote:

"Too often executives and managers stay in their offices and behind their desks. They may hear of conditions in the organizations they lead, but they do not see these conditions for themselves firsthand. Yet there is no substitute for firsthand information and direct contact."

He tried to focus on the positive. In his fireside chat after Pearl Harbor, he didn't talk about the nation's terrible loss. Instead, he said, "The soldiers and sailors who lost their lives will not have died in vain if we remember the lesson the nation learned: Geography alone is no longer a defense against war.

"It is our obligation to our dead — it is our sacred obligation to their children and to our children — that we never forget what we have learned."

While relentlessly positive, he was realistic as well. After he declared a bank holiday, he told the public:

"I do not promise that every bank will be reopened or that individual losses will not be suffered, but there will be no losses that possibly could be avoided. And there would have been more and greater losses had we continued to drift."

FDR was a hands-on executive who organized his staff so that it was filled with people who held diametrically opposing views. That way, FDR made sure conflicts were brought to him for final decisions.

"I'm an old campaigner and I love a good fight," FDR said. "Judge me by the enemies I have made."

Roosevelt was extremely goal oriented. Fighting and winning World War II, he kept saying, was not "an end unto itself."

As American forces were landing on French beaches, FDR was already working to assure that the world after the war was viable. "A sound postwar economy is a major present responsibility," he said in June 1944, when he signed the GI Bill of Rights.

Wrote Axelrod: "FDR was determined not to win this second war only, for a second time, to lose the peace that followed it."

39

Mustafa Kemal Ataturk
Father Of Turkey
Focused On The Future

Mustafa Kemal Ataturk felt that only the mediocre try to please everyone.

The man who founded modern-day Turkey and served as its first president argued that greatness inspires just the opposite.

"Greatness means that you won't try and please everyone, that you won't deceive anyone, that you will discern the true idea for the country, that you will strive for it, that everyone will turn against you and will try to make you change your course," he said to a fellow army officer.

"They will pile up endless obstacles in your path, and you will surmount them, knowing all the time that you are not great, but little, weak and resourceless, a mere nothing, and that no one will come to your aid."

Kemal (who took on the name Ataturk, or "Father of Turkey," later in life) created Turkey out of the remnants of the Ottoman Empire. Not only did he create the state, but he also brought it into the 20th century, introducing reforms like women's rights, educational opportunities and religious freedom for all faiths.

Learning From War

Mustafa Kemal Ataturk (1881–1938) was born in Salonika in what is now Greece. His father was a customs officer and entrepreneur who died when Mustafa was young.

Still, his mother was determined that her son would get a good education. He attended military school as a child and graduated from both the Ottoman War College and Staff College. He liked the military. It "reinforced in him an already masterful disposition," wrote Andrew Mango, author of "Ataturk."

Kemal's life was impacted by a war his country fought with Greece while he was in high school. The Ottoman Empire won easily, but the great powers of the time intervened and prevented it from reaping the rewards of its victory.

"The lesson, that the European great powers intervened when the Ottomans won, but failed to intercede when they were defeated, was not lost on him," noted Mango. Rather than get discouraged, Kemal fueled his nascent nationalism with the new knowledge.

Once graduated from the staff college as a captain, he wanted to be posted where the action was. He'd been part of a group of soldiers who were unhappy with the government, but, much to his disappointment, he was stationed away from the other revolutionary officers.

Yet sometimes, he learned, bad news isn't always as bad as it seems at first. And good things happen to those who wait.

The soldiers posted together took power after a coup in 1908. "But when that first group failed and destroyed itself and the Ottoman state, Kemal and his friends had their chance to prove their worth — and took it," wrote Mango.

Kemal was assigned to the Ottoman outpost in Syria, where troops were more concerned with looting than keeping order. When he was offered a share of the spoils, he turned it down — in part because he was honest but also because he kept his eyes (and morals) firmly planted in the future. "Do you want to be today's man or tomorrow's?" he asked a colleague who was also offered some booty. When told tomorrow, Kemal responded, "Then you can't take the (looted) gold. I have not taken it, nor can I ever."

As a soldier, Kemal felt a strong sense of duty. Although he didn't agree with the sultan, he fought for his country. Take the time he was sent to Africa to protect the Ottoman interest in Libya. It was hopeless, but Kemal went anyway, noting that he'd do his best even if his side was assured of losing.

While he was an optimist, Kemal was also a realist and knew that a deft compliment often paved the way with others. When a fellow officer and would-be revolutionary was denounced for "subversive talk," Kemal praised the local commander's patriotism. Flattered, the local commander agreed that the officer wasn't a traitor.

He stayed focused on his goal at all times — freedom for Turks. That determination helped power his defense of the country. He won widespread acclaim at the battle of Gallipoli, where Ottoman forces repulsed superior Allied troops and sank several British naval vessels.

Kemal still strove for more. At one point, as the most successful officer there, he insisted that all the forces along a particular front be put under his command. Asked if that was too much responsibility, he replied: "On the contrary, it is not enough."

He pushed himself hard, often sleeping just a few hours a night. He pored over dispatches, and he kept a constant stream of messengers busy while he communicated with his subordinates.

After World War I, Kemal took charge of the decimated Ottoman army. It had little respite; over a four-year period it had to repel enemy armies that tried to invade at the same time Kemal was fighting the army of the ruling sultan.

While he was willing to keep fighting, Kemal understood the importance of timing. With the invaders battered by the Turkish ferocity, he saw it was time to start negotiation. He called other leaders to sit down with him and talk about the future.

In 1923, Turkey signed the Lausanne Treaty with Britain, France, Italy, Greece and others. Shortly thereafter, the Turkish Republic was proclaimed, and Kemal was named its president.

He was 42 and had achieved his ambition. Now he wanted to build on his position so he could bring Turkey into the modern world.

He believed in acting fast. Years earlier, as a young officer, he wrote: "If ever I acquire great authority, I think I would introduce in a single stroke the transformation needed in our social life. I do not accept and my spirit revolts at the idea entertained in some quarters that this can be done (only) gradually."

Eyes Wide Open

While Kemal pushed through a series of reforms, he didn't do so blindly. He'd been planning what he'd do for years. As much as a decade earlier he'd discussed abolishing the veiling of women, educating them and allowing them into professions.

He introduced changes in the civil and penal codes, putting them on a European rather than Muslim model. He eliminated Arab script, which had been used in Turkey for thousands of years, and introduced the Latin alphabet.

He made education from grade to graduate school free, co-educational and secular.

He pushed young people to learn about the arts and sciences so that they were well armed to help their country grow.

40

Adm. Chester Nimitz
Inspiration And Teamwork
Helped Him Snare Victory

Chester Nimitz faced a daunting task. As commander of the Pacific Fleet during World War II, he had to serve as the link between Adm. Ernest King — commander of the U.S. Fleet — and three of the most bullheaded men of the war.

Their nicknames said much about who they were and what Nimitz faced. They were Adms. William "Bull" Halsey, R.K. "Terrible" Turner and Holland "Howling Mad" Smith.

Nimitz was known as a nice guy who tried his best to get along with everyone. He went into the situation determined to work out the toughest conflicts with fair negotiation. He was unfailingly polite. But he could get tough.

"He was an absolutely ruthless bureaucrat who was crafty," said professor Robert Love at the Naval Academy in Annapolis, Md. "And no one disliked him. Nimitz was given a coterie of fairly violent personalities to deal with, and he only had to sack one of them."

That was the lesser-known Adm. Robert Ghormley, who Nimitz thought was failing in the sea defense of Guadalcanal in 1942. Nimitz looked for a tougher leader who would follow his instincts, and he replaced Ghormley with Halsey.

Tale Of Teamwork

It was his unerring drive to get subordinates to work together that made him a success. He used it first to rein in those three enormous egos.

Not an easy task. But Nimitz patiently listened to each man and took notes in their meetings. He'd comb over the notes looking for similarities among the men and point those out when talking to them. Soon he had them cooperating.

Nimitz (1885–1966) was born in Fredericksburg, Texas a few months after his father died of heart and lung diseases. His mother and grandfather raised him until his father's brother, William, married his mother when Chester was 5.

The family moved to nearby Kerrville, where Nimitz spent more time around the St. Charles Hotel, which an aunt owned. He was a friendly child and a good student.

He worked long hours at the hotel and had plenty of time to study guests. In 1900, impressed by the demeanor and uniforms of a pair of West Pointers who stayed at the hotel, he sought admission to the Army's elite training college. But his local congressman steered him instead to Annapolis.

After months of study that began before 4 a.m. each day, Nimitz passed the entrance exam and was admitted to the Naval Academy class of 1905.

Nimitz was a top student. Although he and his entire class were sanctioned for hazing underlings, he spent hours each day cracking his books.

He graduated in 1905, at the age of 20, and was assigned duty aboard the battleship Ohio.

Man Of Action

Nimitz set his sights on commanding a fleet. Nearly every move he made was done with that goal in mind. He honed his strategic skills, reading reams of books on history's greatest military strategists.

When Nimitz reached his goal, he took risks, albeit calculated ones. He integrated aircraft carriers into formations; they had been steaming outside of fleet formations because of the extra room they needed to launch planes into the wind. With new circular formations of ships surrounding the carriers, all could easily turn with the flattops so they could both function and be protected by destroyers and cruisers.

To better unite his sailors, he ordered the uniforms of reservists be made identical to those of sailors and officers on active duty. "With no observed differences, the reservists were more easily integrated into full service," wrote naval historian E.B. Potter in "Nimitz."

Nimitz distinguished himself in World War II. Taking command of the Pacific Fleet just three weeks after Pearl Harbor, he deftly rebuilt a fleet disabled in the surprise Japanese attack.

When dealing with those in command at Pearl Harbor, Nimitz realized that if he laid the blame at anyone's feet, that person would be ruined and the Navy would lose any talent that was left at that station. While blame could be handed to anyone connected with the attack, Nimitz asked all of the armed forces' senior talent at Pearl Harbor to remain. The action boosted dangerously low morale there.

"These acts were typical of Nimitz," wrote historian Samuel Eliot Morrison. "And morale, which had reached an all-time low, rose several hundred percent."

Morrison said Nimitz was no patsy, "but a realist of long views with an immense capacity for work, and an equal talent for obtaining the best work of others."

Naval historian Donald Mitchell wrote that "Nimitz's legacy was to reassure his naval and Marine forces in a difficult rebuilding process. Nimitz knew that if he kept his focus on the positive, so would those who followed him."

"His calm assurance of final victory helped restore the faith of the Navy in its own power and ability," Mitchell wrote in a biography of Nimitz for the World Book Encyclopedia.

Ignored Critics

Nimitz also knew that final victory would come only if he took a fully ready naval force to sea against the Japanese. Despite heated criticism from Congress, Nimitz waited until his men were ready to fight before committing forces.

The preparation led to the U.S. victory at the Battle of Midway.

The battle from June 4 to June 6, 1942, crippled the Japanese navy and turned the tide of the war. Four Japanese aircraft carriers and a heavy cruiser were sunk. The U.S. lost a destroyer and the aircraft carrier USS Yorktown.

It was the first major naval victory for the U.S. in the war. With it, the Japanese lost a chance to open a base from which they could again attack Hawaii.

Nimitz later presided over the final Pacific engagements. It was on his flagship, the USS Missouri, that the Japanese signed the surrender documents that ended World War II in 1945.

Nimitz became chief of naval operations after the war and retired from the Navy in 1947.

He headed a U.N. commission that ended a dispute over Kashmir. He remained committed to peacekeeping until the end of his life.

41

Adm.
William F. "Bull" Halsey
Bucked Conventional Wisdom
To Help Win The War

With the U.S. reeling from the surprise attack on Pearl Harbor in December 1941, naval leaders needed to strike a blow that would stall the Japanese advance in the Pacific and restore American morale.

Vice Adm. William F. Halsey, commander of the aircraft carrier USS Enterprise, had the answer: Ignore conventional wisdom.

Halsey directed his force deep into the Japanese-held Marshall Islands in January 1942 and launched an early morning airstrike almost within rifle shot of enemy air and naval bases. Over nine hours, the Enterprise launched 21 airstrikes, inflicting heavy damage on Japanese ships and planes.

"The reason we brought off these early raids is that we violated all the rules and traditions of naval warfare," Halsey wrote in his autobiography "Admiral Halsey's Story." "We did the exact opposite of what the enemy expected. We did not keep our carriers behind the battle; we deliberately exposed them to shore-based planes."

Risk Taker

Halsey, who earned the nickname "Bull," brought the heat of battle to the enemy instead of engaging it at sea. He took risks when the potential reward was great, and his aggressiveness paid off.

Halsey's fleet played a critical role in turning the tide of World War II, helping to halt the Japanese advance and taking the battle all the way to Tokyo. He began the war as a vice admiral, and in 1945 became one of only four men to attain the rank of five-star fleet admiral.

Halsey (1882–1959) took quick action after sizing up a situation.

"If any principle of naval warfare is burned into my brain, it is that the best defense is a strong offense," Halsey wrote. He cited a favorite quotation from Adm. Lord Nelson before the Battle of Trafalgar: "No captain can do very wrong if he places his ship alongside that of an enemy."

When U.S. forces were struggling against the better-equipped Japanese to hold their position on Guadalcanal Island in October 1942, Adm. Chester Nimitz decided to replace the commander in charge there with Halsey. His task of fighting off a Japanese assault on the U.S.-held airfield on Guadalcanal was a key to keeping American supply lines open and the South Pacific campaign going.

Halsey fought for what he believed in, and he had supreme confidence that the valor and ability of his men would surpass that of the enemy. He refused to let his men believe they'd fail. He was quick to praise and encourage and equally quick about disparaging the enemy, sometimes viciously.

Nimitz told reporters that "Bill Halsey is worth a division of battleships," wrote James Merrill in his biography of Halsey, "A Sailor's Admiral."

The Japanese were trying to deliver enough men and firepower to Guadalcanal to expel the American troops from the airfield. Halsey had to block the bigger Japanese fleet. In some of the fiercest naval battles of the war, Halsey's fleet, with air support from Guadalcanal, prevailed.

In the five-day battle, Japan lost 16 ships with nine damaged. The U.S. lost 10 ships with seven damaged. It was a decisive U.S. victory. Japan never seriously threatened the American position on the island again, and the U.S. seized the offensive.

Halsey earned the praise of Gen. Douglas MacArthur: "The bugaboo of many sailors, the fear of losing ships, was completely alien to his conception of sea action."

Go For The Gusto

Halsey became the Navy's go-to guy in a crisis because he threw himself into each challenge with gusto.

That's the spirit that helped Halsey, the son of a Naval Academy instructor, when he was trying to win an appointment to Annapolis. Beginning at age 15, Halsey recalled in his autobiography, "We wrote to every politician we knew and many we didn't know. I had already written even to President McKinley."

After two years of trying, Halsey decided that if he couldn't get into the Navy as a cadet, he would as a doctor. He enrolled at the University of Virginia to study medicine before receiving an appointment from McKinley the following spring.

Halsey thought that nothing beat experience when it came to leading. At age 52, Halsey became the oldest person to win Naval Aviator's Wings, having pushed for the chance to fly even though he couldn't pass the eye exam.

"With a carrier command ahead of me, I wanted a clear understanding of a pilot's problems and mental processes," Halsey wrote. "My eyes still could not pass the tests for a pilot, and how I managed to become classified as one, I honestly don't know yet, and I'm not going to ask."

"Anything can be achieved with the right amount of effort," Halsey believed.

"Take his last month of flight instruction. During that month," Halsey recalled, "I'd fly a fighter, then rush down to the beach and fly a patrol plane, then rush back to the fighters again. Between the first of the month and the 28th, I spent more than 80 hours in the air."

In assuming command in the South Pacific against a better-equipped enemy, Halsey inherited a perilous situation, but he didn't make excuses. Instead, he focused on getting the job done.

Gen. Archie Vandegrift, who was commanding the Marine division on Guadalcanal, told Halsey, "I can hold, but I've got to have more active support than I've been getting."

Halsey, who was working with the equivalent of "a rusty nail and a frayed shoestring," as he later described it, promised to provide everything he could. With the Allied strategy to defeat Germany first and then face down Japan, the South Pacific forces had to make do with what was available.

Only days after Halsey took command, the Battle of Santa Cruz left one of his carriers crippled and other ships damaged. "Despite the losses," Halsey wrote Nimitz, "it will be my utmost endeavor to patch up what we have and go with them."

While Halsey reminded Nimitz of the pressing needs in planes, ships and men, he stressed, "We are not in the least downhearted or upset by our difficulties, but obsessed with one idea only, to kill (the enemy), and we shall do it."

After Guadalcanal, the next obvious target in the Solomon Islands was Kolombangara, a Japanese stronghold. But Halsey didn't do the obvious.

Instead, he attacked the enemy at points of weakness and hit the next island, Vella Lavella, where the Americans encountered little resistance.

Then he cut off Kolombangara from Japan's supply lines.

"The strategy, which was repeated on several occasions, saved lives (and) made maximum use of limited resources," biographer Merrill wrote.

Halsey ran a tight ship, but he earned the undying loyalty of his men by treating them with respect. He relied heavily on their decision-making and tried to keep regulations to a minimum. He called sailors by their first names and permitted officers to forgo their neckties.

"During a break in fighting in the Solomons," wrote Merrill, "Halsey confronted one of his commanders, Arleigh Burke, who had sent a destroyer to Sydney, Australia, over Halsey's objection."

"Sir, my boys haven't had any beer or whiskey for months," Burke explained.

Halsey relented: "All right, Burke, you win. Your boys have been doing a great job, and I can't condemn you for going out on a limb for them."

"That's when I knew," recalled Burke, "I would follow Admiral William Halsey anywhere in this world and beyond."

Halsey was promoted to five-star fleet admiral (one of only five men to have held that rank) in December 1945. He retired from active duty with the Navy in 1947, becoming the president of International Telecommunications Labs Inc.

After he died, he was buried in Arlington National Cemetery, next to his father, Capt. William Frederick Halsey.

42

Egyptian President Anwar el-Sadat
Restored National Pride And Won The Support He Needed To Make Peace

The late Egyptian President Anwar el-Sadat had a decision to make. His driver, who'd worked for Sadat's predecessor, Gamal Abdel-Nasser, stopped at a crossroad to ask whether he should go right or left.

"Which way did Nasser go at this point?" Sadat asked.

"Left," said the driver.

"Signal left and go right," said Sadat.

The story, true or not, is meant to show a trait that contributed powerfully to Sadat's political success, says Jon Ackerman, a Middle East specialist for the U.S. government's Institute of Peace. Sadat (1918–81) understood symbolism.

He knew that his legitimacy depended on his inheriting Nasser's political mantle, and he acted in the name of Nasserism even as he rid Egypt of Nasser's previous pro-Soviet government, says Ackerman.

His most far-reaching symbolic gesture — the one that fixed his place in history — was his trip to Jerusalem and speech to the Knesset, the Israeli legislature.

"The crowning glory of Sadat's understanding of symbolism is that Israelis still get teary-eyed when describing their shock that he went to Jerusalem," Ackerman said.

Sadat was born to a poor Muslim family and entered the military after high school. He was imprisoned for anti-British activities, but he later described that experience as productive because it allowed him time to read and think.

After his release from prison, he ended his arranged marriage to a village woman. He met and married Jehan Safwat Raouf, the educated daughter of an Egyptian mother and British father, whom biographers describe as a strong supporter of her husband's political ambitions.

He returned to the military, where he participated in the movement that took British-backed King Farouk off the throne and put Nasser in power. Sadat was named vice president of the government in large part because he was seen as harmless and no threat to Nasser, says Ackerman.

In that position, Sadat slowly rose to power but was dismissed as insignificant by many of his colleagues in the Foreign Ministry.

"Sadat was systematically underestimated for three decades. He labored long in Egyptian political circles, and he was always just outside the important meetings," said Ackerman.

Sadat was a man who could endure difficulties and bide his time. If he was ever discouraged, no one knew it. And when he succeeded Nasser in 1970, Egypt began to change.

"His opponents had underestimated his aptitude. I think Israelis also had underestimated him," said Ahron Klieman, a professor of diplomacy at Tel Aviv University in Israel.

Advantage Of Surprise

Being underestimated gave Sadat an edge. When he did act decisively, he had the advantage of surprise.

As president, he consolidated his power within the Egyptian government and expelled the country's Soviet advisers. This was the first step on the path to cooperation with the U.S. that eventually resulted in Egypt's being the second-largest recipient of U.S. foreign aid after Israel.

After cutting Egypt's ties with the former Soviet Union, Sadat did something only a deeply self-confident leader could do.

He waged war against Israel.

Sadat restored national pride in 1973 when the Egyptian military, no match for Israel's, nonetheless crossed the Suez Canal and planted the Egyptian flag on soil Israel had occupied. This was a psychological victory for Egypt, wiping out its humiliating defeat in the 1967 war.

"It was not an objective decision; it was a visionary decision," said Shibley Telhami, the Anwar Sadat professor for peace and development at the University of Maryland and author of "Power and Leadership in International Bargaining: The Path to the Camp David Accords."

Sadat knew his people wouldn't trust him to make peace if he didn't restore the honor they lost in the 1967 Six-Day War, Telhami said.

Unafraid to take risks, Sadat saw a different opportunity in 1977 and seized it. He went to Israel, where he was met at the airport by the Israeli military leaders he'd fought.

No Arab leader had ever chosen to recognize Israel, much less go there, address the Israeli parliament and offer terms of negotiation and peace.

His risk paid off. In the negotiations that followed, Egypt regained every inch of the Sinai it had lost to Israel in the 1967 war, and Sadat won the praise of much of the world.

Klieman says that by coming to Jerusalem, Sadat succeeded in converting himself from Israel's worst enemy into a man respected as courageous.

When being photographed at that time, Sadat again showed his understanding of images and symbolism. The picture seen around the world was of the Egyptian president in profile, a proud leader resplendent in a white naval officer's uniform.

A year after addressing the Knesset, Sadat went to Camp David, where he and Israeli Prime Minister Menachem Begin negotiated a peace treaty that changed the political balance of the Middle East and won them a shared Nobel Peace Prize.

Sadat saw the big picture. He drove the advisers at Camp David crazy with his reluctance to read policy papers, says Ackerman. He thought strategically and kept his mind on his objective.

"He was always clear in his mind what he was trying to do," Ackerman said.

Sadat's faith played a large part in his political success. It gave him the capacity to endure, Telhami says.

A religious man, Sadat had a sense of history and destiny. He believed that his cause was right and that justice would prevail. He accepted the role given him by God — that's the way he interpreted it, says Telhami.

But Sadat was not a hero to all. On Oct. 6, 1981, he was assassinated by Islamic extremists who threw grenades and fired rounds of weapons into the viewing stands where he stood to salute army officers at a military parade.

43

Eleanor Of Aquitaine
Her Boldness Molded History

There was only one way to tackle a problem in Eleanor of Aquitaine's view: Find a way to solve it.

The medieval queen of both France and England, "despite her technical status as her husband's property," took charge of her own life, wrote Zoe Kaplan in her biography, "Eleanor of Aquitaine." Historians agree that Eleanor was one of the key political figures of the 12th century. Without her, Richard the Lion-Hearted might not have reigned in England, and there might not have been a Magna Carta.

Eleanor (1122–1204) was born in the Duchy of Aquitaine, a large cultural center that covered ¼ of present-day France. Her father, Duke William X, encouraged her to stretch her mind.

"Unusually, Eleanor was taught to read, and was carefully educated," wrote Andrea Hopkins in "Six Medieval Women."

William took her out on periodic tours of his land to conduct duchy business. As heir to the duchy and aware of her future responsibilities, Eleanor would sop up all she observed — how her father treated his vassals, how he solved legal problems and how he handled ceremonial duties.

She "possessed a sharp intelligence and an interest in learning," Kaplan wrote. "In an age when intellectual interests were the exception rather than the rule, Eleanor stood out in her pleasure in acquiring knowledge."

William X died in 1137, and 15-year-old Eleanor became the duchess of Aquitaine. She was quickly married to Louis VII, who became king of France later that year when his father died. But

Eleanor wasn't happy with her new groom. To her way of thinking, Louis didn't pay enough attention to his kingdom.

In 1147, Eleanor accompanied her husband on the Second Crusade, but counseled Louis to head home early and abandon the quest. Although he did, their marriage was all but over. On their return in 1149, she pleaded with the pope for an annulment — a request that was denied. It became clear during the next several years that Louis and Eleanor's managing styles were different; he preferred prayer, and she preferred taking action. Three years later, with Louis VII's agreement, the pope ended the marriage.

Patroness Of The Arts

Shortly thereafter she married Henry, duke of Normandy and future king of England. It was as Henry's wife that she came into her own. Recognizing the importance of literature and the arts, she established a cultural center in her new domain. Poets and artists flocked to her. She encouraged innovation, and a new literary form, poetic chivalry, emerged.

Seeing that many social gaffes occurred at court by accident because people didn't understand others' customs, Eleanor set up the "Courts of Love," or rules of conduct, from which stem many modern politeness practices.

Aware that people are more loyal when they have contact with a leader, she traveled often, with the king and alone. She met with subjects, and she spent days sorting out local problems in the name of the king. She was confident in her ability as an administrator, but ever mindful that subjects needed to see their rulers as a seamless unit.

Whenever she settled a problem, she reminded subjects that it was their king who'd been gracious.

"Unusual for a woman at the time, she substituted most effectively for the king in his absence as a judiciar, or judge, both in England and France," Kaplan wrote.

When her husband proved unfaithful, Eleanor left him in 1169. It was an unprecedented move at the time. "Such behavior was so extraordinary for a woman, even Eleanor of Aquitaine, that people in Paris and London talked about nothing else," Kaplan wrote.

Rather than sulk, she became proactive and set up a plan to reclaim the glory of her duchy. In her book, also titled "Eleanor of Aquitaine," historian Marion Meade noted:

"Her husband actually imprisoned her for several years to prevent her plan from working. But Eleanor refused to give in."

When Henry II died in 1189, Richard I (the Lion-Hearted) was his heir. Richard, raised by his mother in Aquitaine, hadn't spent much time in England, and in fact disliked it there. The English knew this.

Eleanor confronted the problem head-on. She began a public relations campaign to assure that his subjects welcomed him when he came to England. She ordered grain and game to be distributed in Richard's name.

Still beloved by the British, she then had all the high nobles and clergy who flocked to her new court in London swear their allegiance to Richard. She arranged a general pardon for all those arrested by Henry — with the proviso that those freed must first swear loyalty to her son.

She held off on the coronation, which normally would've been held immediately on his return. Instead, to assure that Richard wouldn't be considered an interloper or foreigner, she toured the countryside with him for two weeks to allow him to greet his subjects.

Matchmaker

Eleanor focused first on what she believed was necessary — sometimes at great personal sacrifice. Richard wasn't married at age 33 and didn't seem in any hurry. Eleanor knew this was unacceptable for the country's continued stability.

So at age 70, she found him a bride, and the two of them traveled across the Alps to Italy and south to Sicily, where Richard was encamped for the winter with the armies of the Third Crusade.

Eleanor knew persistence would win out. She refused to leave until the nuptials were arranged.

Returning from the crusade, Richard was kidnapped and held hostage by Leopold, duke of Austria, who demanded a king's ransom of 100,000 marks of silver — the equivalent of some $10 million today.

When she heard the news, Eleanor set her priorities. Most important was finding where the king was being held. She dispatched emissaries throughout Europe to find her son. Then she raised the needed funds. Finally, though advanced in years, she left for Germany's Rhine Valley to arrange for the release. But complications ensued.

Henry Hohenstaufen, the Holy Roman emperor, added a condition: Richard would have to renounce the British throne and pay homage to him. This was, as Meade wrote, "a calculated humiliation that would have made Richard a vassal of the Holy Roman Empire."

Most advisers urged him to refuse. Eleanor, however, surveyed the situation and figured out that the request was insignificant.

"Quick to realize the meaninglessness as well as illegality of the required act, Eleanor made an on-the-spot decision," Meade wrote. "According to Roger of Hoveson, Richard 'by advice of his mother Eleanor abdicated the throne of the Kingdom of England and delivered it to the emperor as the lord of all.' "

Richard was released, returned to England and reassumed the throne.

Age Is Just A Number

Her political life wasn't over. Following Richard's death in 1199, her son John assumed the throne. Though near 80, Eleanor wouldn't let her age slow her down. As late as the year 1200 she undertook a diplomatic mission to Spain and periodically met with King John in Rouen, France, and elsewhere to provide political advice she'd gleaned from her experience.

But these were treacherous times. Her grandson Arthur made a power play and attacked a castle where she was staying. He demanded that she surrender immediately and turn over all her possessions to him.

Despite her advanced years, she showed tremendous courage under fire — and a sense of humor. According to an anonymous historian who wrote "Histoire des ducs de Normandie," she told her grandson:

"She would not leave and that he should leave at once . . . for he could easily find many other castles to attack than the one she was in."

Eleanor proved to be one of John's strongest advisers. It was she who first urged him to form a pact with his barons to strengthen his rule. Although he refused while she was alive, in 1215 he finally agreed and granted the Magna Carta, the basis of the English Constitution and one of the most revolutionary documents of all time.

44

Statesman
Simon Bolívar
Dedication to Independence
Made Him "El Libertador"

In June 1819, Gen. Simon Bolívar, president of the new republic of
Venezuela, had one main objective.

He wanted to liberate the neighboring state of Colombia —
then known as New Granada — from the oppression of Spanish
colonialism. How would he do it?

The towering Andes Mountains, as well as hundreds of miles of
swamp, stood between his army and Colombia, and the Spanish had
fortified the major passes.

To Bolívar (1783–1830), none of it mattered. He'd do whatever
was necessary to succeed.

To slip past the Spanish mountain outposts, he hired Indian
guides to find secret routes. Then, with his soldiers swearing they'd
rather die than recross the mountains, Bolívar marched them through
the night of Aug. 6, 1813, and defeated the surprised Spanish forces
at Boyaca in the morning.

Bolívar had confidence in his success all along.

"I swear before you," he told a friend in Rome in 1805, "I swear
before the God of my fathers . . . that I shall not rest until I have
broken the chains (of the Spanish)."

That level of determination helped make Bolívar one of the central figures in the independence drive of South American nations. From 1812 to 1824, Bolívar headed the revolutionary movements of modern-day Venezuela, Colombia, Ecuador, Peru and Bolivia, leading to his nickname "El Libertador."

A Taste For Liberty

Bolívar's tutor, Simon Rodriguez, first told Bolivar of the injustices of Spanish rule and cruel treatment of slaves and Indians. Rodriguez also passed on to Bolívar the love for liberty he admired in the recent French Revolution.

Later, Bolívar would thank Rodriguez for his open-minded approach to teaching.

"You have molded my heart for liberty and justice, for the great and the beautiful," Bolívar wrote Rodriguez. "You cannot imagine how deeply your lessons impressed themselves into my heart."

When talk of independence flared in Venezuela in 1806, Bolívar tried to encourage the sentiment. Knowing that an open defiance of the system could be dangerous, he often dampened his words in a veil of polite social banter.

At a toast at the Spanish governor's house in Caracas, he said: "I lift my glass for the happiness of the king of Spain. However, I raise it even higher for the freedom of Venezuela and all of (the Americas)," according to "Simon Bolívar: Latin American Liberator," by Frank de Varona.

When Napoleon took over Spain in 1808, Spanish colonies in South America seized the opportunity to revolt. Realizing that outside aid would greatly further the cause, Bolívar traveled to England to rally support. Although the British government declined assistance, Bolívar made sure to establish connections with many people he thought could help him.

To strengthen his knowledge, he sought out the brightest thinkers of the day. To gain the regard of foreign nations, he persuaded the well-respected leader of two 1806 Venezuelan revolts, Gen. Francisco de Miranda, to return to Venezuela with him.

Knowing that the momentum of a fight could shift on the slightest sign, Bolívar was quick to address his people when an earthquake devastated Caracas in 1812. The common people took the disaster as a sign against their revolution, but Bolívar refused to let them believe it.

"If nature opposes us," he said to them, according to "Simon Bolívar: South American Liberator," by David Goodnough, "we shall fight against her and force her to obey us."

Proactive Approach

Instead of staying distraught after the failure of the revolution, Bolívar — escaping to Cartegena, New Granada — sought ways to improve. So he wouldn't forget his findings, he wrote out the reasons the revolution failed and what to do about it next time.

Seeing that popular support from neighboring New Granada would be instrumental in further incursions against the Venezuelan Spanish, Bolívar published his writings there. To raise the concern of readers, Bolívar warned that their newfound independence could vanish as easily as Venezuela's.

Bolívar knew the value of taking initiative. As a colonel in New Granada's army, Bolívar was ordered to hold his position as others attacked outlying Spanish forces. When he saw an opportunity, however, Bolívar attacked on his own, seizing several towns and recruiting hundreds of additional soldiers to the cause.

The government soon rewarded him for his success, despite his breaking of orders, making him a brigadier general and strengthening his forces.

To encourage loyalty, he gave his men credit when they earned it. Once, when the citizens of Bogotá gave him a laurel after the city's liberation, Bolívar tossed it toward his troops.

"These soldiers are the men who deserve it," he said.

Despite liberating Caracas in 1813, Bolívar lost it to the Spanish again in 1814. Refusing to accept defeat, he launched another attack from Jamaica in 1816. When this attempt failed as well, Bolívar simply tried again — a fourth time. This became the successful campaign over the Andes in 1819.

During his years in exile, he'd devoted himself to his goal of Venezuelan freedom. To keep the revolutionary fervor of the people alive, he continued writing pamphlets and papers, urging unity against Spain. When he saw that his countrymen needed help, he hired soldiers from Europe to support them.

Most of all, he believed in the strength of the will of the people.

"A people that loves freedom will in the end be free," he said.

If he saw that the will of the people was against him, however, he was willing to change his mind. After victories in Venezuela, New Granada and Ecuador established the Republic of Gran Colombia in 1819, Bolívar wanted to annex Upper Peru as well.

Instead of subduing local assemblymen upon hearing they wanted their own independence, Bolívar let them vote, and for their thanks, they named their new country Bolivia.

It was 1825, and Bolívar had finally succeeded in clearing the Spanish from the South American continent.

Throughout the long struggle, he often remembered the words of Alexander Petion, then president of Haiti, written to Bolívar after the failed rebellion of 1816.

"You have failed," wrote Petion. "Such things happen; you will succeed."

45

President
Andrew Jackson

Dedication To The Common Man
Took Him To The Top

Andrew Jackson didn't believe in running from a fight — even when he knew he was completely outgunned.

As a 13-year-old in the Revolutionary War, Jackson was captured by the British and ordered by an officer to clean the mud off his boots. Jackson knew that was wrong. He looked at the officer and said, "Sir, I am a prisoner of war and demand to be treated as such." The enraged officer flailed at the youth with his sword. Jackson bore scars from the wounds on his hand and head for the rest of his life. But he regretted nothing — he'd spoken his mind, and he always would.

"He had a fine intuitive sense of when to scold — and also when to soothe — which in large measure explains why he made such a fine politician and president," biographer Robert V. Remini wrote in "Andrew Jackson."

Jackson (1767–1845) was that rare politician who really was born in a log cabin. The son of Scottish-Irish parents, he grew up in the Waxhaw District on the border between North and South Carolina. Orphaned at 14, Jackson worked briefly as a saddler. Later, his courage, duty and cunning helped him become a successful lawyer, general and politician.

As the nation's seventh president, he expanded the powers of the office while seeking to deal fairly with the common man. "He became the classic example of the self-made man vaulted from log cabin to the White House all on his own," Remini wrote. "He was the personification of the American success story."

Ambitious Enterprise

Jackson's mother had hoped he'd become a Presbyterian minister, but he liked life on the wild side: gambling, horse racing, cockfighting and drinking. But Jackson eventually took stock of his life. Would those activities get him ahead? He realized they wouldn't, and so he began pursuing a teaching career at age 17.

Teaching didn't satisfy his growing ambition, however, so he decided to study law. It offered more of a challenge. While apprenticing, he tried to smooth his rough frontier edges. He carefully watched other lawyers to see how they dressed and spoke. He then modeled his attire and manners on theirs. He took dancing lessons so that he could socialize with others. When business proved scarce in North Carolina, Jackson didn't hang around — he headed west with friends to the newly settled frontier town of Nashville.

Hard work, determination and courage won him a reputation as a lawyer who delivered. Tall, erect, with a shock of fiery red hair and deep-set blue eyes, Jackson immersed himself in his work. In his first month in practice he succeeded in collecting 70 debts from deadbeats who'd routinely scoffed at repaying loans. Demand for his services boomed, and he handled more than a quarter of the legal cases in the county in his first five years in business.

Intensely loyal, Jackson wasn't afraid to stand up to anyone who insulted his family or friends. He'd go as far as fighting a duel if someone were insulting enough. Yet he was quick to forgive an enemy. Jackson was once wounded in the arm during a duel with Thomas Hart Benton. Later, both men served in the U.S. Senate, and Jackson befriended him. Benton became one of Jackson's strongest supporters, helping him win elections and push programs through Congress as president.

Jackson was elected Tennessee's first congressman in 1796. He moved to the Senate the following year, but he returned to Tennessee to protect his holdings when a bad land deal and the panic of 1797 nearly ruined him. As he did with every event, Jackson learned from it — he decided that paper money and banks had to be treated with great care and not a little distrust.

Leading an army of frontiersmen-volunteers during the War of 1812, Jackson wanted to make sure he had his men's respect. So rather than isolate himself from them, he did everything they did — sharing their quarters, eating the same food and sharing their hardships. His toughness earned him the nickname "Old Hickory."

Jackson won a stunning victory at New Orleans — even though the American military foundered during much of the war — because he was unafraid to break with tradition.

With his usual pragmatic idealism, he used Jean Lafitte and his local band of pirates to help defend the city, even though he called them "hellish banditti." He also enlisted a regiment of free black soldiers over the objections of local whites. Both groups served with distinction.

It was considered unseemly for presidential candidates to campaign, but Jackson did so anyway. For example, he marched in a parade in New Orleans to celebrate the anniversary of his historic victory. He beat John Q. Adams resoundingly in the next election.

Innovative Thinker

As president, Jackson saw that a different approach was needed than that of the Founding Fathers to keep up with the dynamic and growing country. Instead of behaving like an elitist, Jackson always tried to keep the common man's viewpoint in mind. He believed in pure democracy, and he often stopped to listen to an Average Joe's opinion when he was out and about.

That approach wasn't always successful, however. The near riot at his inaugural celebration at the White House showed the down side — a mob broke dishes and glasses and muddied furniture while Jackson escaped out a side door.

His brand of democracy promoted the government as honest umpire, offering the hope of equal access and protection to all. Jackson broadened the power and scope of the executive office, using more vetoes than all of his predecessors combined to get his way.

His democratic instincts and suspicion of paper money flared when the charter of the Second Bank of the United States approached renewal. Jackson complained that the quasi-public bank, which he called "a hydra-headed monster," used government money to confer favors on its wealthy friends. When Nicholas Biddle, the bank's patrician president, responded by squeezing credit and terrifying business owners, Jackson blamed him for the financial panic.

Jackson acted quickly. He vetoed the bank's recharter and withdrew government funds. He lobbied members of Congress hard to close the bank, sometimes cajoling and sometimes haranguing them. It worked — Jackson beat the bank.

He often toiled far into the night, and he tried to be as accessible as possible. Jackson often invited Cabinet members and their families over in the evening so the men could get work done while the women and children visited and played nearby.

Jackson easily won a second term in 1832, although the fractious battle over the bank diminished his popularity. Declaring "debt incompatible with real independence," he became the first and last president to pay off the national debt and distribute the excess revenues to the states — during an election year.

Twenty thousand spectators heard his farewell address in 1837, when the mood differed remarkably from that attending his first inauguration. "Eternal vigilance by the people is the price of liberty," Jackson warned his audience, "and you must pay the price if you wish to secure the blessing." The crowd stayed respectfully silent.

PART 6

Motivating Others To Victory

©Bettmann/CORBIS

We shall fight on the beaches, we shall fight on the landing grounds, we shall fight in the fields and in the streets, we shall fight in the hills; we will never surrender.

— WINSTON CHURCHILL

46

Statesman
Winston Churchill
He Put His All Into The Effort
To Win World War II

When Hitler's armies invaded Russia in June 1941, British Prime Minister Winston Churchill threw his support behind the retreating communist forces.

Many of Churchill's fellow politicians didn't like it. But Churchill, himself staunchly anti-communist, knew that political differences needed to be cast aside in the face of a common adversary.

"If Hitler invaded Hell," said Churchill, as cited in "The Churchill Wit," edited by Bill Adler, "I would make at least a favorable reference to the Devil in the House of Commons."

Knowing that only a combined effort would defeat the Axis powers, Churchill set out to gather other world leaders to help Britain. Before the U.S. entered World War II, he persuaded President Franklin D. Roosevelt to lend cruisers to protect British merchant ships from German blockades, and he met with leaders as distant as China's Chiang Kai-shek.

Back home, Churchill sought out members of the opposition Labor Party to serve in his Cabinet in order to gain support from the working class for the war effort.

Churchill was determined to do everything he could to win the war. After almost four more years of tireless effort, Churchill got his reward when Germany surrendered on May 8, 1945.

Changing The Equation

Although Churchill (1874–1965) came from a wealthy background, he wasn't the picture of a young man destined for success. He was a poor student, and his grades soon began to hold him back when he twice failed the entrance exam for Sandhurst, the British military college.

Realizing that his dream of joining the military was on the verge of collapse, Churchill resolved to pass on his next try. He joined a cram school and studied old exam questions late into the night until he knew the material backward and forward.

With renewed confidence, he passed the entrance exam.

Although he graduated from Sandhurst into the 4th Hussars cavalry regiment, he knew his earlier failures in school made him deficient in knowledge compared with others his age.

To raise himself to the level of his peers, he began to re-educate himself at age 22. According to "Churchill's England" by Adele Gutman Nathan, he used his spare time to read histories of the world, and then he tried to mimic in his own writings the well-rounded sentences and powerful words he read.

Churchill knew he needed firsthand experience with a subject to speak knowledgeably about it, so he began traveling extensively to get it. By 25, he'd covered revolts in Cuba for a British newspaper and participated in military conflicts in Egypt and South Africa.

"Twenty to 25," he later wrote. "Those are the years! Don't be content with things as they are."

When Churchill joined the House of Commons for the Borough of Oldham in 1900, he tempered his early speeches, knowing that it wouldn't be wise for a freshman member to make enemies. But as his speech-writing talents grew, so did his confidence and his stature in Parliament.

Understanding that powerful words could sway others to his viewpoint, Churchill began preparing four to five days before a speech was scheduled. To make sure he knew his material, he studied all available figures and readings, as well as speeches others had made on the topic.

To hone his style, he spent hours writing a speech. If a precise word wouldn't come to him, he stopped writing until it did. Sometimes he sat waiting for more than 10 minutes. If he was away from his desk when the right word came, he made a note of it and later incorporated it into the speech.

Once the writing was done, he stood in front of a mirror, watching himself recite a speech over and over until he had the words and gestures memorized. Then he tested it on friends to get their comments.

By the time he delivered his speeches formally, Churchill had them down so well that many thought he simply made them up on the spot.

He used long pauses to increase the drama of his words. Although many thought he was simply deciding what to say next, the hesitations were planned.

"Those pauses are just part of my trade," he said in "My Dear Mr. Churchill" by Walter Graebner. "I always — well, most of the time — know exactly what I am going to say, but I make believe, by hesitating a little, that a word or phrase has just come to me."

Knowing that an unprepared speech could tarnish his image as a great speaker, Churchill always avoided impromptu debates. If somehow cornered and forced into one, he kept his replies short and simple.

By the later part of his career, he had become so skilled that he commanded fees of up to $50,000 per speech.

Be Prepared

In charge of the British Navy before the start of World War I, Churchill had closely watched Germany and warned his colleagues of impending war. Few believed him. Instead of going with the consensus, though, he trusted his own judgment and began to prepare the navy anyway.

To make sure the navy was ready, Churchill visited warships, and he learned gun sizes, the number of guns and men, and even how the men were trained and fed. He got to know the senior officers and then helped convert the ships' fuel source from coal to the more efficient oil. To counter the firepower of the big battleships the Germans were building, he equipped British ships with heavier guns than ever before.

Although some called his moves foolish, Churchill stuck to his plan.

"Any clever person can make plans for winning a war if he has no responsibility for carrying them out," he countered.

When the war suddenly broke out in Europe in July 1914, the navy was the only prepared branch of the British military. After keeping tabs on the movements of the German forces, Churchill had secretly ordered his warships to battle stations weeks before. British ships were ready to help transport troops across the English Channel to reinforce the French, as well as to hunt German subs in the North Sea.

Seeing how men were mown down when they tried to move out of trenches, Churchill ordered his engineers to build armored cars to smash over the trenches. (When these first "tanks" appeared at the Battle of the Somme in 1916, they were still the property of the navy.) His approach helped change the way war was fought.

Churchill also saw that air power would be key to future warfare, and so he started the Naval Air Service. His few scrappy planes even managed to destroy six German zeppelins.

During World War II, Churchill knew the success of his country in the Battle of Britain lay in the courage of the people. Britain had to fight alone during that time, from June 1940 through May 1941, against massive German air raids including the London Blitz. So Churchill worked hard to boost the people's morale with the tools he had — his words.

His speeches on radio and in Parliament helped give the British strength against the nightly bombing, even as half of London lay ravaged by fire. To give people hope, he visited bombed-out towns and consoled the homeless. "We shall defend our island, whatever the cost may be," he said in 1940. "We shall fight on the beaches, we shall fight on the landing grounds, we shall fight in the fields and in the streets, we shall fight in the hills; we will never surrender."

47

Naval Giant
Horatio Nelson

He Inspired His Men
And Great Britain To Glory

Not many of us have had to stop Napoleon, destroy two fleets and lead an armada from a shell-torn deck in the midst of a punishing broadside. But England's Vice Adm. Horatio Nelson did all those things and gloried in it.

It wasn't just that he was a fearless and brilliant tactician who stunned his enemies with the unexpected.

Nelson (1758–1805) rose to become Britain's greatest hero largely because he led his men to believe they could be great. He constantly looked for ways to awaken them to the glory of their service and his heroic vision of the British Navy.

One story clearly conveys what came to be known as the "Nelson touch."

When he was still a captain, Nelson once was faced with a midshipman who was too frightened to scale the masts. Rather than berate the man, Nelson challenged him with a smile.

" 'Well, Sir, I am going (to) race to the masthead, and beg I may meet you there,' " Nelson said, according to Lady Hughes, a contemporary quoted in Roy Hattersley's "Nelson."

"No denial could be given to such a wish," she continued, "and the poor fellow instantly began his march."

"His Lordship never took the least notice with what alacrity it was done, but when he met at the top, instantly began speaking in the most cheerful manner, and saying how much a person was to be pitied who could fancy there was any danger, or even anything disagreeable, in the attempt.

"After this excellent example, I have seen the timid youth lead another, and rehearse the Captain's words."

A captain in Nelson's fleet once wrote: "He is so good and pleasant that we all wish to do what he likes, without any kind of orders."

Victory At Trafalgar

That willingness to serve him was key to Nelson's victory at Trafalgar, where he destroyed any chance of Napoleon Bonaparte's invading England.

Nelson thought the mental and physical health of his men was as important as his weapons, supplies or ships. "It is easier for an Officer to keep men healthy, than for a Physician to cure them."

When Nelson took command of the fleet before the Battle of Trafalgar, the men were bored, and their morale was low.

To get them working together toward a common end, he had them all paint their ships in the yellow-and-black Mediterranean style of his HMS Victory.

At sea, he always made sure his men were on the ready, keeping them alert by varying their chores and even alternating the routes they took between voyages.

Perhaps most important, he understood the benefit of informing every man — from his best officers to his cabin boys — of his goals and battle plans.

They'd perform most effectively, he realized, if they knew what they were trying to achieve.

Nelson prepared for whatever might happen in battle, exploring every possibility of achieving his objective with his officers. They were so thoroughly prepared that in battle they didn't have to waste time figuring out and signaling their course of action. They already knew.

He constantly sought to innovate. In fact, he was famous for doing what the enemy least expected and what tradition frowned upon.

At the Battle of Trafalgar, for example, Nelson broke one of the navy's oldest rules: Never divide your forces. Instead, he stunned the French and Spanish armada by breaking his force into two columns.

His ideas didn't flow just one way.

Nelson liked to dine with seven or eight of his officers at a time. Weather permitting, he'd sit down with the captains of other ships on a rotating basis. He ate sparingly, focusing his attention on the discussion. He took care to talk to each person.

Thanks largely to those evenings, his men became a band of brothers — a cohesive fighting unit conscious of each other's strengths and weaknesses.

He was known as a careful listener — even at social occasions.

"Even at the jovial board, and in the height of unrestrained merriment, a casual suggestion, that flashed a new light on his mind, changed the boon companion into the hero and the man of genius; and with the most graceful transition he would make his company as serious as himself," wrote Samuel Taylor Coleridge, a secretary for one of Nelson's captains.

Nelson, the son of a humble preacher, knew he needed to work harder than his peers to develop leadership skills. Unlike others, he didn't have ties to higher-ups. Promotion in the British Navy often depended on political or familial connections.

He studied his superiors carefully, adopting the tactics of his strongest leaders. He modeled his encouraging stance after a senior officer who used confidence-building to get excellent results.

Braving Every Danger

Nelson decided early on to make the ideal of "King and Country" his own. He told himself: "I will be a hero, and confiding in Providence, I will brave every danger."

When an opportunity arose to take a risk for greater success, he never wavered. Life for him was as a choice between "cypresses or laurels" — between failure and death or success and glory.

"If a man consults whether he is to fight when he has the power in his own hands, it is certain that his opinion is against fighting," Nelson said.

Nelson didn't just seek victory; he wanted to crush the enemy.

When he was a captain in 1795, he was part of a battle in which 14 British ships faced down 17 French ships. The British fleet captured two of the French vessels and drove off the rest.

But that wasn't good enough. He wrote his wife that had the British taken 10 French ships, still, "I could never have called it well done."

Nelson disciplined his body to help discipline his mind. He never slept more than two or three hours at a time, learning to think clearly with little sleep.

When he wasn't poring over maps, he walked the upper decks for six to seven hours a day, sometimes through the night, conjuring ever more cunning ways to destroy the French.

After Nelson died in the Battle of Trafalgar, Robert Southey, a contemporary biographer, wrote in his "Life of Nelson" that his death "was felt in England as something more than a public calamity; men started at the intelligence, and turned pale, as if they had heard of the loss of a dear friend."

Such was the Nelson touch.

48

Emperor
Napoleon Bonaparte
How He Conquered Europe . . .
And Surrendered It To Ego

He was a turnaround artist par excellence.

In little more than 10 years, from 1799 to 1809, Napoleon Bonaparte pulled France from the chaos of its revolution and made it Europe's dominant power.

The career military officer did so with one key strategy: inspiring fierce loyalty in his citizens and troops.

How? By making his victories theirs.

"You have rushed like a torrent," he told his troops after they crossed the Italian Alps. "You have overthrown, dispersed and scattered everything that opposed your advance.

"Such success has brought joy to the heart of *your* country; there *your* fathers, *your* mothers, *your* wives, *your* sisters, *your* sweethearts are rejoicing in your success and proudly proclaim that they belong to you."

Said historian Maurice Hutt, "Napoleon knew there is a limit to what coercion can achieve; belief, opinion and loyalty cannot be brought into existence by exhortation or command."

Instead, Napoleon (1769–1821) inspired awe — even through the bitter cold of his Russian campaign, his troops starving, their feet wrapped only in rags.

According to one soldier's account, "The emperor had turned his head toward us as he passed. He seemed, in this hour of misfortune, to inspire us by his glance with confidence and courage. We forgot all our miseries and thought only of the emperor."

No Time Like The Present

Napoleon also motivated himself and his troops with a sense of urgency.

"For me there is always at stake . . . my very existence and that of the whole empire," he said. "I simply cannot afford to let anyone threaten me without striking back."

Fired up, his soldiers raced across Europe with a speed unmatched by any of his opponents. The passion of his troops, rushing headlong, overwhelmed and splintered opposing forces.

Napoleon, born the son of a Corsican public servant, subdued the royal houses of Spain, Germany and Italy.

But once victorious, he acted quickly to win the loyalty of his new subjects.

He told his stepson, Eugene, whom he'd made viceroy of Italy: "Show respect for the nation you govern, and show it all the more as you discover less grounds for it.

"Learn their language; frequent their society; single them out for special attention at public functions; like what they like; approve what they approve."

"But above all," he said, "the less you talk the better. Silence is often as effective as a display of knowledge."

Napoleon prepared for battle by preparing for the worst.

"I purposely exaggerate all the dangers and all the calamities that the circumstances make possible," he said.

But once he laid out his strategy, he stuck with it. Stubbornness, he believed, went a long way.

He often spoke of the Battle of Austerlitz he won against Austrian forces in 1805. "I did not doubt that (they) would end up yielding me ground," he said. "And it was this conviction which made me stand firm." On the fifth day of the French assault, the Austrian forces retreated.

His trick to quelling anxiety was realizing that a chance meeting with death could end it all at any minute. "(So) it is stupid to worry about anything," he said.

And he was equally forceful in squashing limiting thoughts. "Something becomes impossible," he said, "only if you decide it is.

"The impossible is the specter of the timid and the refugee of the coward. . . . The word (impossible) is only a confession of impotence."

His self-confidence was based on his voracious study of military history.

If Alexander could conquer provinces from Greece to India, Julius Caesar from Judea to Stonehenge and Attila the Hun from Mongolia to ancient France, then he could surely conquer Europe, he concluded.

"The reading of history very soon made me feel that I was capable of achieving as much as the men who are placed in the highest ranks of our annals," he wrote. "What seemed to present difficulty to others to me appeared to be simple."

Too Much Confidence

But his faith in his own brilliance was too unwavering. And his commitment to a set direction was too absolute.

Napoleon rarely listened to the advice of ministers and generals when they contradicted him.

"I have never wished to be anyone's man," he said. "I am my own minister. . . . It is I who conduct affairs. Probity, discretion and action are all that I demand of a man."

Indeed, he had to whittle down the importance of anyone near him who might even partially usurp his position, one observer noted. The smallest mishap, the slightest negligence, sent him into a fury.

From the outset of his reign, "he reduced his ministers to the levels of clerks," said historian Hippolyte Taine. "Any sign of independence annoyed him. Toward the end, the only people he tolerated near him were people who were virtually his slaves."

With no humility or moderating influence to anchor him, he determined to conquer Russia, ignoring the warnings of several advisers.

He not only attacked but did so knowing his troops would be deep within Russia through the dead of winter. Setting out with half a million soldiers, he returned to France with 10,000.

Having refused to cut his losses, he'd allowed his soldiers to be drawn farther and farther into the Russian heartland. Czar Alexander's soldiers staged guerrilla attacks and adopted a slash-and-burn defense, destroying crops and shelter — anything the French troops could use to survive.

Napoleon met his final defeat at Waterloo in 1815.

49

Sir Bernard Law Montgomery

This Commander Made Sure To Put His Men First

From Gen. Dwight D. Eisenhower to the lowliest private, they called him "Monty."

And that's the way Bernard Law Montgomery liked it.

Though he was the leading British commander during World War II, Montgomery encouraged informality. Among officers, he thought it made them more comfortable speaking their minds to him. And the men in the trenches had earned it, he believed.

That conviction came from his own nearly fatal experience as a young officer in the trenches of World War I. Shot in the chest in 1914, he recovered and returned to the French battleground in 1916.

The way he survived left its mark. "My life was saved that day by a soldier of my platoon. I had fallen in the open and lay still, hoping to avoid further attention from the Germans. But a soldier ran to me and began to put a field dressing on my wound; he was shot through the head by a sniper and collapsed on top of me."

Through the rest of his military career, he planned, planned and planned some more to minimize deaths and maximize the prospect of victory. That approach helped him pound Nazi Gen. Erwin Rommel twice during World War II and later become the deputy supreme commander of the North Atlantic Treaty Organization.

Montgomery (1887–1976) believed that firsthand was the best way to get information, including on the battlefield. He railed against the senior officers' living "in comfort, which became greater as the distance of their headquarters behind the lines increased." In World War II, "Monty" was never far from the front lines.

Or far from his men. Rather than strut about with ribbons on his chest, he wore a tattered sweater and beret. When he talked to the troops, he didn't address them from a podium. He gathered them to him, more a football coach than an aloof general.

One of those who saw Montgomery's egalitarian streak firsthand was Arthur Harris, head of the RAF's bomber command during the war. They went to staff college together in 1927.

Harris wrote after World War II, "In Monty we certainly had a soldier who knew his onions, no matter what the 'high-ups' in the army might officially think of the smell."

After fighting at Dunkirk in 1940, Montgomery was sent by Churchill to Africa to take over a failing campaign against the Nazis' Africa Corps. His mission? Outfox the cunning Desert Fox, Rommel.

Montgomery knew that appearances send a message, so he sent soldiers and supplies to the south to make Rommel believe the British army's full strength was there. He built dummy tanks and a dummy pipeline and disguised the real tanks in the north as trucks.

With characteristic insight, Montgomery saw the importance of the task. "The battle which is about to begin will be one of the most important battles in history. It will be the turning point of the war."

It was.

The Battle of El Alamein in Egypt set a new course for Britain and the Allies. Churchill, who'd belabored Montgomery for a slow start, later said, "Before Alamein we never had a victory; after Alamein we never had a defeat."

Firm Convictions

Montgomery was born to an Anglican bishop father and a rigid Victorian mother. They demanded upright behavior from him; later, he'd insist on the same from himself.

He strove to lead from the time he was young. He was confident in himself. Knowing he excelled at sports, he insisted on being team captain at school. That same determination and focus in the army led him to quick promotion.

Later in his career, British and American peers would find his convictions grating. He frequently clashed with Eisenhower, Lt. Gen. George Patton and even his own government.

But his critics knew that he got results, especially in the turning-point battles of North Africa and Sicily. If he thought he was right, he spoke his mind in no uncertain terms.

"His outstanding characteristics were his professional thoroughness," wrote historian Alan Palmer, "and the projection of his self-confidence so as to arouse enthusiasm among his troops."

Montgomery knew the element of surprise gave him the upper hand, so he studied his opponents carefully. Anticipating their moves, he'd do the opposite. He opted for slow, methodical movement of troops when allies and enemies alike expected a rapid advance. Or he'd argue for a blow to the jugular when others planned on a broad sweep.

Montgomery said, "The commander must decide how he will fight the battle before it begins. . . . He must make the enemy dance to his tune from the beginning and not vice versa."

Even one of Rommel's generals praised Montgomery. "He is the only field marshal in this war who won all his battles. The decisive factor is the organization of one's resources to maintain the momentum."

Montgomery's dedication to organization and surprise tripped up Rommel. It also led to a clash with Eisenhower.

Montgomery wanted a lightning strike on Berlin in September 1944 to end the war faster, with fewer dead. Eisenhower feared, wrongly as it turned out, that rear-guard Nazi troops would form an Alpine fortress. Ike opted for a broad front and gave Montgomery only limited support for a less powerful thrust on Berlin.

Montgomery's underpowered Operation Market Garden failed. It became known as "a bridge too far."

But Ike had seen Montgomery's strength. He wrote in a report, "He loves the limelight, but in seeking it, it is possible that he does so only because of the effect upon his own soldiers, who are certainly devoted to him."

Eisenhower added, "I have great confidence in him as a combat commander. . . . Like all other senior British officers, he has been most loyal — personally and officially — and has shown no disposition whatsoever to overstep the bounds imposed by Allied unity of command."

Tough Optimism

Montgomery took on the toughest jobs with optimism. On D-Day, June 6, 1944, he led the British and Canadian units. Their grim job was to take on the main force of the German army.

They might not have liked Montgomery, but U.S. generals praised him. Writing about D-Day, Gen. Bedell-Smith, Ike's chief of staff and a Montgomery critic, said, "I don't know if we could have done it without Monty."

Montgomery's success gave U.S. troops the shot they needed to break out from Normandy into the heart of France.

While blunt with his peers and superiors, he was a soldier's soldier. He earned the nickname "the Spartan General."

Historian Michael Howard wrote, "No British commander in the war showed a better grasp of the intricacies of his appallingly difficult profession, and none showed a better understanding of the men that he led."

British historian Nigel Hamilton said Allied success came from Montgomery's remembering history's lessons, especially the horror of the Battle of the Somme in World War I.

Hamilton wrote, "His legacy to the Allied armies endures today: training, rehearsal and professionalism in the handling of men and women in a democratic cause — guided by the demand for simplicity, clear aims, frontline leadership and care among commanders to preserve human life as far as possible."

50

President Ronald Reagan
This Persistent Populist
Changed American Politics
And Quashed Communism

Ronald Reagan wanted to change the political landscape of America. But first he needed to change the face of conservatism.

To sell his conservative message, Reagan emphasized "forward-looking optimism" in his campaigns for governor of California and president, former Reagan aide Peter Hannaford said.

The conservative standard bearer in the 1960s was Barry Goldwater, who struck most Americans as strident, mean-spirited and dangerous.

"(Reagan) was a populist whose conservatism was based on widely shared American values," said research scholar Dinesh D'Souza, a former Reagan administration domestic policy analyst, in his book "Ronald Reagan: How an Ordinary Man Became an Extraordinary Leader."

Reagan was also a former New Dealer, "and this gave his criticisms of (big) government an authenticity they otherwise would have lacked," D'Souza said.

Changing The Political Landscape

As president, Reagan achieved "an ideological realignment," D'Souza said. "He shifted the political center by changing the terms of the debate. The true test of a political revolutionary is the effect that he has on the other party."

By maximizing his leadership mandates in the presidential elections of 1980 and 1984, "Reagan forced liberalism as an ideology, and the Democrats as a political party, to transform themselves in order to survive," D'Souza said. "Reagan ensured that the effects of his revolution would endure for the long term, because even the opposition adopted his rhetoric and swore fidelity to his main objectives."

Case in point: Seven years after Reagan left office, President Bill Clinton — in his 1996 State of the Union address — reaffirmed that "the era of big government is over."

"That was a line right out of Reagan's playbook," Hannaford said.

By communicating his message with persistence and passion, "Reagan destroyed the New Deal coalition, and laid the groundwork for Republicans to (eventually) become the majority party for the first time in four decades," political analyst William Schneider said.

As president, Reagan, born in 1911 in Tampico, Ill., helped unify the Republican Party by staffing the White House and Cabinet with moderates as well as conservatives. "He believed in the free market of ideas," said David Gergen, Reagan's White House communications director.

Reagan positioned himself as a national political figure in 1976 by challenging fellow Republican Gerald Ford for the party's presidential nomination.

Ford was the incumbent, and Republicans showed few signs of supporting a challenger.

Touting two successful terms as governor of California (1967–75), Reagan opposed Ford's policy of détente; decried the stagflation that marred the domestic economy; and spoke against the Panama Canal treaty that transferred authority of the canal from the U.S. to Panama.

Reagan's first defeat was unexpected: He lost the New Hampshire primary. Ford, a moderate, narrowly won in a conservative stronghold. He also won in Massachusetts, Florida, Illinois and Vermont.

"The consensus within the GOP was that after five losses in a row, Reagan was finished. Republican governors, senators and mayors urged Reagan to withdraw," D'Souza said.

Nancy Reagan urged her husband to quit. So did Reagan's campaign manager, John Sears. Reagan's reaction? "I'm taking this all the way to the convention," he said.

Already deeply in debt, Reagan borrowed additional funds, bought time on local TV stations and aired portions of his campaign speeches.

The result? "Reagan confounded the political establishment by winning the North Carolina primary. He then trounced Ford in several Southern and Western states, where his criticisms of détente and the Panama Canal treaty resonated with Republican voters," D'Souza said.

Ford narrowly won the Republican nomination, with 1,187 delegates to Reagan's 1,070.

During the convention, Reagan rocked the hall with a rousing speech designed to unify the party. "The tumultuous reaction revealed that although many of the delegates were unwilling to dethrone a sitting president, their hearts were with the challenger," D'Souza said.

The persistence that marked his 1976 campaign would become the hallmark of his presidency from 1981 to 1989.

Tenacious Goal-Setter

Reagan came to office with three main goals, recalls Hannaford. "The first was to straighten out the economy and set it on a course for long-term growth. Second, to curb the federal government's rate of growth. Third, to end the Cold War.

"In foreign policy, his strategy was to force the Russians to make a choice: engage in an arms race while throwing their economy into chaos, or negotiate in good faith.

"During his first term they chose an arms race. By the late 1980s, they were near bankruptcy. They had little choice but to negotiate."

The result? "The collapse of Soviet communism," Hannaford said.

Reagan's resolve on economic policy led to the nation's longest peacetime boom to that point. Critics slammed his combination of tax cuts and smaller government during the 1981–82 recession. Reagan persisted. The recovery began in the spring of 1983.

During his two terms in office, the prime interest rate fell from 20% to 10.5%. The inflation rate dropped from 13.5% in 1980 to 4.1% in 1988. More than 17 million jobs were created.

In making decisions, Reagan worked closely with his staff, D'Souza recalls. Labor Secretary William Brock, who was overruled several times in this manner, comments that Reagan was so gracious in deciding against him that Brock never felt a sense of personal rejection or humiliation.

Reagan shaped public opinion to his policies, not vice versa.

"He consulted polls to identify areas where a majority of people disagreed with him, so he could use his power of persuasion to change their minds," former White House pollster Richard Wirthlin said.

Reagan once defined statesmanship this way: "To have the vision to dream of a better, safer world and the courage, persistence and patience to turn that dream into a reality."

Reagan's tenacity, vision and communications skills turned many of his critics into admirers. Two months after Reagan left office, Sen. Edward M. Kennedy (D-Mass.) said in an address to a Yale University audience: "Whether we agree with him or not, Ronald Reagan was an effective president. He stood for a set of ideas. He meant them, and he wrote most of them not only into public law but into the national consciousness."

"He was a persistent fellow who knew what he wanted," reporter Sam Donaldson said. "He came to Washington to change the world for the better, and for the most part he did. There's no one like him on the scene today."

After a 10-year battle with Alzheimer's disease, Reagan died on June 5, 2004. He was 93. In his 1990 autobiography, "An American Life," Reagan wrote, "We had to recapture our dreams, our pride in ourselves and our country, and regain the unique sense of destiny and optimism that had always made America different from any other country in the world." His courage on behalf of the American people will never be forgotten.

51

Gen. Douglas MacArthur
His Focused Was Trained
On Getting The Job Done

In 1943, at the height of World War II, a reporter asked Gen. Douglas MacArthur where his air forces were striking that day.

"Oh, I don't know. Go ask Gen. Kenney," MacArthur answered, referring the reporter to one of his subordinate generals.

The shocked reporter responded, "General, do you mean to say you don't know where the bombs are falling?"

MacArthur smiled and said, "Of course I know where they are falling. They are falling in the right place. Go ask George Kenney where it is."

Wrote Geoffrey Perret, author of "Old Soldiers Never Die: The Life of Douglas MacArthur": "The hallmark of the MacArthur style was high seriousness of purpose combined with a studied informality of style."

It was a combination that allowed MacArthur to spur peak performance in his men when he was Allied commander in chief of the Southwest Pacific Area in World War II and supreme commander for the Allied powers in Japan after the war.

President Dwight D. Eisenhower, the general who served on MacArthur's staff in Washington and the Philippines, recalled in the memoir "At Ease." "When he gave an assignment, he never asked questions; he never cared what kind of hours were kept; his only requirement was that the work be done."

MacArthur (1880–1964) was a hero of two world wars, winning 15 decorations for battlefield gallantry, including the Medal of Honor. During World War II, he inspired hope in millions around the world.

When ordered to leave the Philippines after the Japanese invaded, his promise to the Filipino people — "I shall return" — stirred them to resist the Japanese occupation. His striking image became a symbol of wartime determination.

After the war, he won the hearts of the nation he defeated. Knowing that good relationships are founded on respect, he made sure he treated the Japanese emperor and people with kindness and regard.

Moved Men

The Japanese people at first turned their backs in a show of abject submission when he passed in a car. To encourage a feeling of equality and cooperation, MacArthur taught them to give a friendly wave of the hand instead.

At the same time, he knew that his own regal bearing commanded their respect. He made sure that he was someone they could look up to, which was very important for the Japanese.

In Korea, his boldness kept the Allies from being driven into the sea. His daring Inchon amphibious landing behind enemy lines turned the tide in the Korean War's first year, sending the North Koreans into retreat.

MacArthur possessed an unshakable faith in his own anointing. Like many of the post–Civil War generation, he held a romantic view of life in general and war in particular.

"The soldier, above all other men, is required to perform the highest act of religion — sacrifice," he often told audiences. "In battle and in the face of danger and death, he discloses those divine attributes which his Maker gave him when he created man in his own image."

MacArthur made his name in World War I. He was already well known in the Army because of his father, the late Lt. Gen. Arthur MacArthur. But it was in combat in the Great War that the son earned his own renown.

As chief of staff of the 42nd Infantry Division, MacArthur earned few points with Gen. John J. Pershing, the commander of American forces in France. The 42nd was a sloppy unit, lax in military courtesy and poor at drill and ceremony. But it fought and fought hard, and that's all MacArthur cared about. "Fighting men are the real soldiers," he told a subordinate.

MacArthur, who led his men into battle even as a general, was the only man to survive when his reconnaissance patrol was hit by artillery fire one night. "It was God. He led me by the hand, the way he led Joshua," he said later. To him, that he survived many brushes with death confirmed what he always believed: that God had set him apart to achieve great things.

MacArthur asked no more of his soldiers than he was willing to do himself. In World War II, he repeatedly exposed himself to enemy fire. "The Almighty has given me a job to do, and he will see that I am able to finish it," he told one officer.

Next to physical courage, MacArthur believed the most essential trait of the successful soldier was the ability to communicate. He picked the young Dwight Eisenhower as his assistant because of Ike's writing ability.

MacArthur was a writer — some say a poet even — and a talker. He despised meetings but spent hours each day in impromptu talks with others. New officers were routinely brought into his circle through such talks.

His talking could turn down-to-earth men like Eisenhower into enthusiastic fans. He could even win over hard-bitten critics. After an 11-hour meeting with him in Tokyo after World War II, one critic came away exclaiming, "How does he do it? He's in better health than when I saw him before the war. More fascinating than when he was chief of staff. What a man! What a man!"

MacArthur didn't just argue people into agreement; he inspired them to believe in him and to imagine the world as he did. He understood what his critics didn't: that men are moved to the highest purposes and greatest sacrifices by their emotions.

Back home, cynics poked fun at MacArthur's heroic style of oratory. But he figured out what motivated his listeners, and he focused on that message. Upon his return to the Philippines, for instance, MacArthur told the Filipino people,

"Rally to me. . . . Rise and strike. . . . The guidance of divine God points the way. Follow in his name to the Holy Grail of righteous victory!"

"It was an emotional appeal to an emotional people," wrote Lt. Gen. George Kenney, MacArthur's air chief, in "The MacArthur I Know." "I don't know how it sounded back in the United States, but it was not meant for the people back home. It was meant for the Filipino people, and they really liked it," Kenney said.

What critics saw as self-promotion, MacArthur saw as leadership. People needed a hero to follow, he believed, and they needed to see someone easily recognizable. So he made his style of dress distinctive — a crumpled Philippine field marshal's cap, faded khakis, aviator sunglasses, leather flight jacket and corncob pipe. Few ever forgot the sight.

Won Loyalty

Although he could be shy, MacArthur was warm with subordinates. He greeted them by shaking hands, often placing his left hand on a man's shoulder at the same time. He often put his arm around his favorites and flattered people with exaggerated praise to win their loyalty.

A man of action, MacArthur also tried to arm himself with information. His reading revolved around his profession. He read several newspapers every day and often engaged his staff officers in lengthy discussions of the news. He encouraged debate and discussion and was open to having his mind changed, as long as it didn't involve admitting a mistake.

His warm relationship with Eisenhower soured when MacArthur passed off a mistake of his own as an error by his staff, which then included Eisenhower.

Lofty in his view of the world, he was nevertheless down-to-earth in his regard for the business of battle. He had no patience with routine duties like record keeping and often threw away letters and drafts when he was finished with them.

MacArthur started World War II as an air-power skeptic, but he became a convert when he found airmen such as Kenney willing to fight. He'd handpicked Kenney to command his air forces after other aviation commanders disappointed him.

The pick surprised even Kenney. When MacArthur was Army chief of staff in the early 1930s, he'd clashed often with Kenney, a brash young proponent of air power.

When Kenney asked why he'd been chosen, MacArthur told him, "In time of peace, you need an officer and a gentleman. In time of war, you need a rebel and a son of a bitch."

MacArthur saw himself as transcending both, but with the responsibility for picking the rebels and fighters he needed to win the war.

52

Gen. Norman Schwarzkopf

Solid Dedication To Troops

Makes Him An

All-Time Great

While some of Lt. Col. H. Norman Schwarzkopf's fellow instructors at West Point were glad to be out of harm's way, Schwarzkopf sought the chance to lead and pleaded for a second tour of duty in Vietnam.

And when his opportunity to command a battalion arrived in 1969, he embraced it to the fullest.

His men in the field were the first to notice. After serving under a leader who never left base, their new commander was different: he led by example. Schwarzkopf immediately demanded a helicopter to see his commanders in the field.

The inattention of his predecessor was evident. What Schwarzkopf found was a ragtag bunch who often didn't carry loaded weapons, didn't wear helmets, didn't establish defensive positions and were needlessly putting themselves in danger.

"Things are going to start changing around here, Captain, right now," he recalled telling one company commander in his autobiography, "It Doesn't Take A Hero."

Back on base, with his troops waiting in line in the rain outside the mess hall, Schwarzkopf learned that officers were served in a special section and didn't have to wait. He ended that practice on the spot, taking his place at the end of the line.

While generals and politicians had failed the troops in Vietnam, Schwarzkopf dedicated himself to inspiring his forces with his passionate brand of leadership and, over the next two decades, creating the world's best fighting force.

And in commanding his half-million-strong force to an overwhelming victory in the 1991 Gulf War at the end of his career, Schwarzkopf closed the book on the days when the heroism of America's soldiers was questioned.

Born in 1934 in Trenton, N.J., Schwarzkopf knew the value of personnel. He took care of his people.

In the Vietnam War, when a mine killed or maimed a soldier, Schwarzkopf would fly to the site.

On one occasion in 1970, Schwarzkopf realized his company was in the middle of a minefield, and he stayed behind with them after the helicopter evacuated an injured soldier.

Another mine went off 20 yards from Schwarzkopf. He worried that the screams of the soldier, whose leg was grotesquely twisted, would cause the others to panic and run.

"I realized I had to get over to him and help him," Schwarzkopf wrote. "I started through the minefield, one slow step at a time. . . . My knees were shaking so hard that each time I took a step, I had to grab my leg and steady it with both hands before I could take another."

Schwarzkopf finally reached the man and lay down on him to keep him from thrashing. Even though his own chest was punctured with shrapnel, Schwarzkopf waited until everyone was safe before letting himself be taken to the hospital.

Making The Best Of It

At times in his career, faced with incompetent commanders or dead-end jobs, Schwarzkopf persevered and seized whatever opportunity came his way.

Serving under an alcoholic commander in 1958 was a far cry from what Schwarzkopf had dreamed the Army would be like, and he considered bailing out.

But his new superior convinced him to endure: "There are two ways to approach it. No. 1 is to get out; No. 2 is to stick around and someday, when you have more rank, fix the problems. But don't forget, if you get out, the bad guys win."

In 1978, Brig. Gen. Schwarzkopf was assigned to an assistant staff job at Pacific Command in Hawaii. Here, the West Pointer would serve under a two-star admiral who'd graduated from Annapolis.

Schwarzkopf's Army predecessor, on the verge of a forced retirement, warned him the post would "ruin your career." For months, Schwarzkopf was treated with disdain and relegated to pushing paper.

But Schwarzkopf showed he was a team player and assumed responsibilities his superior let fall by the wayside. Eventually, he handled planning and base negotiations with Korea, Taiwan and Japan. While the admiral focused on grand strategy, Schwarzkopf, without being asked, took over operational and policy planning for potential conflicts.

When Schwarzkopf moved on, he was able to tell his replacement that his job "had been fulfilling, that I'd gained great experience working with the other armed forces, and that serving in the Pacific would not be the end of his Army career."

Schwarzkopf learned from his commanders and drew from their strengths in developing his own leadership philosophy.

Take the time in 1983 when he was given command of the 24th Mechanized Infantry Division at Fort Stewart, Ga., and he was promoted to major general. The night he received the assignment, Schwarzkopf lay in bed and "conjured up my role models — Lathan, Boatner, Warner, Cavazos, Livsey, Vuono" and came up with a list of goals for his command.

"I was eager to introduce everything I'd learned — Vuono-style management reviews, Cavazos-style maintenance programs," Schwarzkopf wrote.

Schwarzkopf believed in lifting people up. In 1984, one of his division's battalions was crushed in a mock battle in the Mojave Desert against an opposing force trained in Soviet tactics.

"If Schwarzkopf had relieved me on the spot, he would have had a perfect justification," the battalion commander recalled in the Schwarzkopf biography "In the Eye of the Storm," by Roger Cohen and Claudio Gatti.

Instead, after a tough critique, Schwarzkopf took the commander aside and put his arm around him.

"I have every confidence that you will bring it together," he said. "But you must be positive with the young officers who feel they let you down and let themselves down."

Innovator

Schwarzkopf was ever willing to question his superiors or reject the accepted way of doing things.

After earning a fourth star and being elevated to commander in chief of Central Command in late 1988, he was supposed to direct war exercises to react to a Soviet incursion into Iran. Thinking such a scenario outdated, Schwarzkopf drew up plans for dealing with an Iraqi aggression instead.

Although the new war plan hadn't been officially approved, Schwarzkopf refused to base the annual war games on the Iran plan in the process of being junked.

Instead, the July 1990 exercises involved a response to Iraq seizing crucial Saudi oil fields. When Iraq invaded Kuwait weeks later, Schwarzkopf was ready with a plan to defend Saudi Arabia.

Schwarzkopf put his faith in good planning — and in his people.

Having drawn up an ambitious ground attack that called for an unprecedented logistical effort, Schwarzkopf knew his commanders would deliver. The key was moving the XVIII Airborne Corps' 117,000 personnel and 28,000 vehicles more than 500 miles in a few weeks to set up a surprise flanking attack.

To maintain the element of surprise, they couldn't move before the air war began and knocked out Iraq's communications.

"Never before in the history of warfare has an army moved so much so far so fast," Cohen and Gatti wrote.

Schwarzkopf's instructions, as one commander recalled: "OK, boys, this is what I wanna do; now you think about this and come back and tell me how I'm gonna do it."

As the air war began, Schwarzkopf delivered the ultimate tribute to his troops: "My confidence in you is total."

53

Queen Elizabeth I
Reason And Moderation
Marked Her Reign
As One Of The Greatest

Q ueen Elizabeth I had the right to demand blind fealty. But the monarch knew better. She could also motivate people by explaining her actions.

To charge up those who worked for her, she offered reasons for her edicts.

When she spoke to the Church of England's senior clergy, she easily might've insisted they enforce uniformity of worship in the country, as she'd mandated, and left it at that. Instead, she explained why: "Religion is the ground on which all other matters ought to take root, and being corrupted might mar all the tree."

As Alan Axelrod, author of "Elizabeth I, CEO: Strategic Lessons From the Leader Who Built an Empire," wrote, "Elizabeth recognized that if you treat the people you work with like robots, . . . they will work like robots. Treat them as intelligent members of a team, and they will not only take an ownership pride in their work, they may well go about it more creatively."

Following her remarks, the clergy approached the task with vigor, subjecting themselves to scathing criticism in the House of Commons. But Elizabeth loyally assured them of her full support.

Her support of loyal co-workers was more than words. When her trusted secretary of state, William Cecil, Lord Burghley, fell ill in 1598, the queen sat at his bedside for hours feeding him broth. Her actions weren't lost on the rest of the court.

Power Of Integrity

For most of her early years, her ascension remained doubtful. Elizabeth (1533–1603; reigned 1558–1603) was the daughter of Henry VIII. Her mother, Anne Boleyn (the second of Henry's six wives), was executed by the king.

Henry was succeeded by his sickly son, Edward VI, who reigned just six years (1547–53) before succumbing to tuberculosis. Edward was succeeded by Mary I, who reigned from 1553 to 1558 and brought the country to the brink of ruin.

Mary reversed the Protestant Reformation encouraged by her father, returning the nation to Catholicism and creating havoc. She persecuted and killed foes, earning the nickname "Bloody Mary." Elizabeth suffered, too, under her half-sister's rule. She was held in some form of custody for most of it, and she was briefly confined to the Tower of London.

Elizabeth learned and profited from these experiences. Falsely accused of complicity in a plot to overthrow her half-brother, Edward VI, she was subject to a withering interrogation from Sir Thomas Tyrwhitt. He convinced himself he could wring a confession from the 16-year-old and get her to implicate others.

He failed. He wrote in a letter in January 1549: "She hath a very good wit and nothing is got out of her but by great policy. She will not confess to any practice by Mrs. Ashley (her governess) or the cofferer (her household manager, Sir Thomas Parry)."

Elizabeth also recognized early on that vengeance wasn't an effective means to an end. When the protector of young King Edward VI later offered to punish anyone who slandered her or spread malicious rumors about her, she declined the offer.

She replied that punishing the slanderers "should be but a breeding of an evil name of me, that I am glad to punish them, and so get the evil will of the people, which thing I loathe to have."

She realized that taking vengeance on the rumormongers wouldn't stop the lies but would make her look power hungry and alienate popular opinion.

Instead, she suggested a more effective way to stop the gossip — an appeal to public opinion through respected authority. She asked the protector and Privy Council to circulate a proclamation through the country declaring the rumors lies and urging people not to spread them.

Balanced Approach

When Elizabeth assumed the throne following Mary's death, she inherited a nation in turmoil. The royal coffers were empty. The nation was in strife with both Scotland and France, and conflict ignited by Mary I could easily have plunged England into religious wars similar to those in France at the end of the 16th century.

Elizabeth revealed how prudent and astute she was. Although she would resurrect the Church of England, she allowed Mary a Catholic burial, a move she felt would be less divisive.

She was also willing to compromise. While she re-established the Church of England and insisted on uniformity of rituals at first, she decided that to insist on full uniformity of belief would only further divide the troubled nation. She refused to make windows into men's souls. "There is only one Jesus Christ, and all the rest is a dispute over trifles," she said.

One of her first acts as queen was to reorganize the Privy Council and lower it to 13 from 39 members to make it more efficient. Although she dismissed numerous advisers loyal to Mary and her policies, she retained several who'd served under the previous monarch, to signal the end of persecution.

Axelrod points out that Elizabeth didn't succumb to the natural tendency of a new leader to sweep away the old order wholesale but wisely chose to emphasize continuity.

Elizabeth demanded absolute loyalty from her advisers, but she didn't surround herself with yes men. She charged members of her Privy Council that "without respect of my private will, you will give me that counsel you think best." Her ability to choose wise advisers was one of her key strengths.

Elizabeth had enough self-confidence to walk out of step with the crowd when needed, however. She lived when women were considered little more than property, and her subjects questioned the ability of even royal women to govern. Yet at an early age, Elizabeth knew her own intellect and made known her intention to use it.

According to Axelrod, Elizabeth at age 13 sent a portrait of herself as a gift to a royal relative along with a letter. In it, Elizabeth wrote: "For the face I grant I might well blush to offer, but the mind I shall never be ashamed to present." The face in the portrait, she noted, could fade with time, "yet the other (her mind and intelligence), nor time with her swift wings shall overtake, nor misty clouds with their lowerings may darken, nor chance with her slippery foot may overthrow."

Elizabeth I would need all her intelligence and confidence to navigate the slippery rock of palace intrigue and to steer England on a course that would make it, in Axelrod's words, "the greatest empire the world has ever known."

She felt it important to move out into the field. Despite great inconvenience (a trip into the countryside involved a procession of 400 wagons and 2,400 pack horses and traveled at most 12 miles a day), Elizabeth went out among the people every summer in trips called "progresses." "We come for the hearts and allegiances of our subjects," she said. "It's easy to become a remote leader cut off from the nitty-gritty realities of the enterprise," Axel rod wrote. "What better way to communicate her affection (and) regard for her people than by direct contact?"

Elizabeth expanded England's territorial claims, with Sir Francis Drake sailing around the world. Her navy (and bad weather) defeated the Spanish Armada in 1588, catapulting England to the status of a leading world power.

Elizabeth's combination of intelligence and shrewdness helped make her reign one of the most glorious times in English history. Under her, the arts and culture flourished. Edmund Spenser, Christopher Marlow, Ben Johnson and William Shakespeare all prospered under her reign, which became known as the "Elizabethan Age."

54

Amnesty International's Ginetta Sagan

She Refused To Be Intimidated In Her Fight To Expose Human Rights Abuses

In prison during World War II, Ginetta Sagan was tortured. When two Germans entered her cell, she anticipated a new round of horror.

As they ushered her into a car, she looked up at the starry sky and thought, "I'll never see another aurora."

But the darkness was followed by a remarkable dawn. The "Nazis" who removed her from prison were actually defectors, working with Italian freedom fighters. They delivered her not to death but to Catholic nuns at a local hospital.

Sagan would survive to become a rescuer herself, helping to launch Amnesty International and Aurora, organizations dedicated to prisoners of conscience like herself and victims of human rights abuse.

Sagan (1923–2000) was born in Italy to parents active in the resistance against the growing tide of fascism and nationalism in Europe. Her father despised Italian strongman Benito Mussolini, and said of Hitler: "That man is going to destroy all of Europe, and then he will destroy himself."

Her parents soon became casualties of Hitler's war. Her mother, a Jew, was sent to Auschwitz; her father, a Catholic, was shot in Italy.

Sagan risked her own life by working as a courier for the Northern Italian resistance. Small and short, she ferried papers to the underground press and disguised herself as a cleaning lady to steal stationery from public offices.

She became known as "Topolino," or "Little Mouse." But the Fascists had set a trap for her. Sent to prison, where thugs abused her, she came close to total despair. But a small act of kindness — one that would animate her activism later in life — sustained her.

A mysterious friend tossed into her cell a bread roll, which contained a piece of paper. "Coraggio," it read — "courage" in Italian. This message, which let her know that she wasn't forgotten, was an inspiration that came to symbolize her lifelong struggle to work for "forgotten prisoners" — ordinary people deprived of their human dignity and freedom.

"It was awful, but I wanted to survive," she said. "I didn't want to disappear like a grain of dust or sand. I wanted to tell the story if I possibly could."

New Life

In America, she did. After schooling stints at the Sorbonne — where she met luminaries such as writer Albert Camus — and the University of Chicago, she married and moved to Northern California.

Former CIA Director William Casey once called her "that housewife from Atherton." It was true: Using her home as a base, she conducted a global campaign to save abused prisoners in regions from South America to South Asia.

She transformed her searing experiences into compassion, drawing on her memories of horror and brutality to commiserate with victims.

Understanding the propaganda of oppression, she approached her task with savvy and sophistication. She knew, for example, not to accept at face value reports from governments that listed deaths as attempted escapes. Mussolini's government had listed her own father's death in that euphemistic category. He hadn't attempted to escape at all. He was told to run, and then he was shot.

Sagan's own resources and determination, however, weren't enough to popularize her cause. She knew she would have to enlist the influential in Amnesty International's work to be effective on a large scale.

"I had all these cases of political prisoners coming in and very few people to help at that time to develop the organization," she said. "I thought, 'Who is going to help? Nobody is going to listen to me.'"

So she decided to recruit a neighbor — the singer Joan Baez, who lived nearby in Woodside.

"I thought I would bring to Joan Baez the case sheets and the Amnesty material and ask her, Would she please help?" Sagan said.

Baez said she would. She not only performed popular fund-raising concerts for Amnesty International but also did considerably less glamorous tasks. "Sometimes people would call me and say that my secretary has such a beautiful voice," Sagan said.

Amnesty International quickly took off. "We traveled to Santa Barbara (Calif.), Los Angeles, Texas, Boston. And in each place, our purpose was to organize and establish a group of people who then could do their work," Sagan said. "By 1976, we had 70,000 members."

Though a darling of the political left — "Human rights begin at breakfast," she would often say to cheers — she also won the respect of Ronald Reagan in the 1980s for her willingness to help political prisoners in communist and socialist countries.

"We must remember them all; we cannot be selective in our outrage," she said. Known as a diligent worker, she spent many years on a 150-page report on human rights abuses in the Socialist Republic of Vietnam, checking and cross-checking her records. Many on the political left were stunned and outraged.

"I was called time after time a 'fascist' and a 'cold warrior' for doing this study of the re-education camps, by some of the same people with whom I worked on human rights issues in Chile, in Brazil, in South Africa," Sagan said.

Some even insinuated that she was a CIA agent. Sixties radical leader William Kunstler went so far as to call her report a "cruel and wanton act," saying, "I do not believe in public attacks on socialist countries, even where violations of human rights may occur."

But Sagan, despite vandalism to her house and other harassment, persisted in her work of exposing abuse. She called herself a meddler, doing the work others found unpalatable.

In 1994, Amnesty International established the Ginetta Sagan Fund in her name to stop torture and help educate the world about human rights abuses, with special emphasis on abuses against women and children.

Sagan received many awards, including Italy's top honor in 1996. In 1998, she gave an invitational address at the Third International Human Rights Conference in Warsaw, Poland.

Before her death, she had the pleasure of meeting with some leaders, such as Poland's Lech Walesa and the Czech Republic's Vaclav Havel, whom she'd worked to free. She'd seen the collapse of the world created in the bloody crucible of World War II. "What more could one hope to see in one lifetime?" she said.

But she insisted that the world remain vigilant, for the cause of human rights never dies.

"As in the past, it is not the evidence of injustice that is lacking — it is the courage to believe in and act upon the evidence to help these victims that is missing," she said. "Silence in the face of injustice is complicity with the oppressor."

55

Genghis Khan
Conqueror Won Wars, Minds

Genghis Khan played — or, more accurately, fought — to win. "Khan recognized that warfare was not a sporting contest or a mere match between rivals; it was a total commitment of one people against another," wrote anthropologist Jack Weatherford in "Genghis Khan and the Making of the Modern World." "Victory did not come to the one who played by the rules; it came to the one who made the rules and imposed them on his enemy."

Khan understood the importance of unity. If conquered people swore fealty to Khan, he brought them into his tribe, encouraging intermarriage and promoting their leaders to positions of authority.

But for those who continued to fight, he could be ruthless. When attacking towns or fortresses surrounded by a moat, he'd force prisoners — sometimes the captured comrades of soldiers still fighting him — to rush forward until their bodies filled the channel, making his assault on a citadel easier.

There was a method to his madness. Khan knew the value of propaganda. His use of terror tactics often preceded him. This created panic among his enemies, who often surrendered without a fight or fled before he arrived.

Khan (1162–1227) was born in the Mongol equivalent of a working-class family. His father died when Khan (born Temujin) was just a youngster. The family's clan then abandoned young Temujin, his mother and siblings on the steppes, leaving them to die.

Temujin and his family refused to give up. They scrounged some food and began building a hut for shelter. And the boy who became Genghis learned from this experience.

"The tragedies his family endured seemed to have instilled in him a profound determination to defy the strict caste structure of the steppes," Weatherford wrote.

Temujin didn't start out a warrior. In a not-uncommon incident for the time, a raiding party attacked his family's settlement and made off with his wife. Khan could have ignored the incident, a perfectly acceptable alternative since the raiding party represented a far superior force than he could muster. Or he could go after her.

"He had to think carefully and devise a plan of action that would influence the whole of his life," Weatherford wrote. Temujin decided to fight. "He would find his wife or he would die trying."

Rather than run blindly into a fight he couldn't win, Temujin planned carefully. First, he met with a powerful local chief. He persuaded the chief to forge an alliance with him. Together, they raided the offending tribe and recovered Temujin's wife.

Despite his reputation as a ferocious warrior, Temujin had a strong sense of integrity and believed in keeping his word. Those around him who didn't often paid a price.

After a nearby tribe, the Jurkin, refused to honor its commitment as an ally and attacked his base when he was away, Temujin acted swiftly.

He called a tribal meeting, called a *khuriltai*, in which offending tribal leaders were tried. Found guilty, "they were executed as a lesson about the value of loyalty to allies, but also as a clear warning to the aristocrats of all lineages that they would no longer be entitled to special treatment," Weatherford said.

Goodwill Gesture

To help heal the pain and anger the Jurkin felt over the incident, Temujin adopted a Jurkish orphan. He thus created a kinship between his Mongol tribe and the Jurkin.

Temujin also understood the value of patience. Typically after an enemy fled, victorious soldiers concerned themselves with looting and let the defeated get away. Temujin saw that gave the enemy an opportunity to reorganize. So he ordered his soldiers to wait until victory was complete before taking any loot.

Recognizing the importance of goodwill, Temujin made sure the widows and orphans of soldiers killed in battle received their husbands' share of the booty. "The policy not only ensured the support of the poorest people in the tribe but it also inspired loyalty among his soldiers, who knew that even if they died, he would take care of their surviving family members," Weatherford wrote.

In 1206, Temujin took the name Genghis Khan, or "fearless leader." With an eye on perception, he didn't assume power dictatorially. He called a khuriltai and made sure he was democratically installed.

With a fierce and loyal army, Khan mapped out stunning new fighting strategies. For instance, he directed one flank to engage an enemy head-on while another flank secretly made its way around the skirmish. Then, to the enemy's surprise, his soldiers would "appear suddenly hundreds of miles behind enemy lines, where least expected," Weatherford wrote.

Knowing he needed more than fighters to stage successful raids, Khan employed his own engineering corps to build what his soldiers needed. He instructed them to use available materials to build weapons such as siege engines. That way, he avoided having to transport heavy equipment.

Aware that information was his greatest weapon, Khan sent out scouts who mapped every hill and valley. He wanted to be prepared for every contingency.

To better lead his men, he broke the army into manageable groups. The army was set up in groups of 10 men to form a squad. Each squad was combined with nine others to form companies of 100 and then battalions of 1,000 and divisions of 10,000. By creating these massive units that crossed familial and tribal boundaries, Khan "broke the power of the old-system lineages, clans, tribes and ethnic identities," Weatherford said.

Practical Principles

Khan was practical, and he sought to head off problems before they occurred. He forbade the selling of women, a common practice at the time. He made rustling a capital offense. Anyone who found an animal had to return it to its owner. He decreed religious freedom for everyone and even exempted religious leaders and properties from taxes.

He understood that as his empire grew — at its height it covered much of Asia and parts of Eastern Europe — communications became increasingly important. He created an early version of the Pony Express, ordering that fresh horses be held ready every 25 miles for messengers. He also made administrators adopt a writing system that allowed the government "to record the many new laws and to administer them over vast stretches of land now under his control," wrote Weatherford.

Khan insisted that everyone take part in his society, either in the military or some form of public service. If they didn't fight, wrote Weatherford, "they were obligated to give the equivalent of one day of work per week for public projects and service to the khan."

Credits

"President Dwight D. Eisenhower: Hard Work And Delegation Helped Him Steer Our Nation," by Christopher L. Tyner, was originally published in *Investor's Business Daily* on Aug. 24, 2001.

"Founding Father Thomas Jefferson: His Reputation Was Built On Hard Work, Education And Humility," by Michael Mink, was originally published in *Investor's Business Daily* on July 3, 2002.

"Rome's Julius Caesar: Total Focus On His Goal Made Him Emperor," by Michael Richman, was originally published in *Investor's Business Daily* on May 11, 1999.

"Prime Minister Margaret Thatcher: Her Principled Determination Turned Britain Around," by Claire Mencke, was originally published in *Investor's Business Daily* on Dec. 18, 2001.

"Sgt. Alvin York: This Soldier Aimed To Please," by James Detar, was originally published in *Investor's Business Daily* on Dec. 20, 2002.

"Bishop's Grit Gave Him Wings: Fighter Ace Was Short On Natural Skill, But Long On Passion," by Peter Benesh, was originally published in *Investor's Business Daily* on Dec. 2, 2002.

"Calvin Coolidge: Quiet President Worked For Limited Government," by Charles Oliver, was originally published in *Investor's Business Daily* on Dec. 4, 2001.

"President Theodore Roosevelt: He Relied On Persistence To Overcome Obstacles," by Nick Turner, was originally published in *Investor's Business Daily* on Dec. 21, 1999.

"Sam Houston: His Disciplined Strategy Secured Texas For The Nation," by Paul Katzeff, was originally published in *Investor's Business Daily* on Jan. 23, 2004.

"President Harry S. Truman: He Gave His All," by Christopher L. Tyner, was originally published in *Investor's Business Daily* on Oct. 8, 2001.

"Gen. George S. Patton: He Led With Boldness And Clear Intentions," by Charles Oliver, was originally published in *Investor's Business Daily* on May 6, 1998.

"Statesman Yitzhak Rabin: His Push For Peace Made Him A World Figure," by Kathryn Linderman, was originally published in *Investor's Business Daily* on Aug. 28, 2000.

"Confederate Gen. Robert E. Lee: Troops Rallied 'Round His Principled Leadership," by Susan Vaughn, was originally published in *Investor's Business Daily* on April 15, 1999.

"Gen. Colin Powell: Climbed To The Top By Always Doing His Best," by Curt Schleier, was originally published in *Investor's Business Daily* on May 26, 1999.

"American Indian Leader Tecumseh: His Honesty And Character Brought Tribes Together," by Scott S. Smith, was originally published in *Investor's Business Daily* on April 14, 1999.

"Soldier-Statesman George Marshall: Winning The War And Peace," by Jed Graham, was originally published in *Investor's Business Daily* on Jan. 8, 2004.

"John Pershing: Dedicated General Led Charge From The Philippines To Europe," by Ken Hoover, was originally published in *Investor's Business Daily* on Jan. 29, 2004.

"President Abraham Lincoln: His Focus Helped Him Preserve The Union," by Amy Reynolds Alexander, was originally published in *Investor's Business Daily* on Dec. 31, 1999.

"Aviator Billy Mitchell: His Efforts Helped Build A Separate Air Force," by Daniel J. Murphy, was originally published in *Investor's Business Daily* on Dec. 3, 1997.

"Gen. Benjamin Davis: He Proved His Heroism In Face Of War And Racial Prejudice," by Michael Mink, was originally published in *Investor's Business Daily* on July 25, 2002.

"Ahmed Shah Massoud: The Lion of Panjshir Roared Against Oppression," by Peter Benesh, was originally published in *Investor's Business Daily* on Sept. 9, 2002.

"Gen. Ulysses S. Grant: His True Grit Helped End The Civil War," by Michael Mink, was originally published in *Investor's Business Daily* on July 17, 2002.

"Czech Leader Vaclav Havel: Dissident Writer Dedicated His Life And Words To Political Change," by J. Barnes, was originally published in *Investor's Business Daily* on Oct. 16, 2000.

"Liberator Toussaint L'Ouverture: His Drive For Freedom Charted The Path To Haiti's Independence," by J. Barnes, was originally published in *Investor's Business Daily* on April 18, 2001.

"Statesman Nelson Mandela: He Persevered Against Apartheid — And Won," by Cord Cooper, was originally published in *Investor's Business Daily* on July 19, 1999.

"Sitting Bull: A Warrior Only By Necessity," by Murray Coleman, was originally published in *Investor's Business Daily* on Feb. 9, 2004.

"First Lady Eleanor Roosevelt: Her Dedication To Helping Others Made History," by Shana Smith, was originally published in *Investor's Business Daily* on Jan. 22, 2004.

"Alexander The Great: This Innovative Strategist Inspired His Soldiers To Conquer An Empire," by Susan Vaughn, was originally published in *Investor's Business Daily* on March 1, 1999.

"President George Washington: Father Of Our Nation Pushed For Success," by Mike Angell, was originally published in *Investor's Business Daily* on May 29, 2002.

"Emperor Constantine The Great: He Studied Others To Become The Best Administrator Of The Ancient World," by Brian Mitchell, was originally published in *Investor's Business Daily* on Sept. 23, 1999.

"Aviator James H. Doolittle: Careful Preparation Helped Turn The Tide In World War II," by Claire Mencke, was originally published in *Investor's Business Daily* on May 4, 2001.

"Indian Emperor Akbar The Great: Rethinking Old Ways Strengthened His Rule," by Scott S. Smith, was originally published in *Investor's Business Daily* on Jan. 12, 2000.

"Bold Military Strategist Karl von Clausewitz: His 10-Volume Battle Plan Elevated This General To The Rank Of Expert," by Michael Mink, was originally published in *Investor's Business Daily* on Feb. 19, 2004.

"Rear Adm. Grace Murray Hopper: Her Determination Helped Computerize Defense," by Kathryn Linderman, was originally published in *Investor's Business Daily* on March 14, 2001.

"OSS Founder William Donovan: His Careful Study Helped U.S. Gain Intelligence Lead," by Jim Christie, was originally published in *Investor's Business Daily* on Aug. 27, 1999.

"Military Strategist John Boyd: His Bold Tactics Changed The Way We Fight — And Win," by Joseph Guinto, was originally published in *Investor's Business Daily* on Sept. 25, 2003.

"Activist Lech Walesa: His Resolve To Change The System Without Violence Helped Free Poland," by Michael Richman, was originally published in *Investor's Business Daily* on July 26, 2000.

"President Franklin D. Roosevelt: His Straightforward Approach Lifted America From Fear," by Curt Schleier, was originally published in *Investor's Business Daily* on May 14, 2003.

"Mustafa Kemal Ataturk: Father Of Turkey Focused On The Future," by Curt Schleier, was originally published in *Investor's Business Daily* on Feb. 12, 2004.

"Adm. Chester Nimitz: Inspiration And Teamwork Helped Him Snare Victory," by Dan Moreau, was originally published in *Investor's Business Daily* on Feb. 14, 2002.

"Adm. William F. "Bull" Halsey: Bucked Conventional Wisdom To Help Win The War," by Jed Graham, was originally published in *Investor's Business Daily* on Dec. 29, 2000.

"Egyptian President Anwar el-Sadat: Restored National Pride And Won The Support He Needed To Make Peace," by Sheila Riley, was originally published in *Investor's Business Daily* on March 12, 2001.

"Eleanor Of Aquitaine: Her Boldness Molded History," by Curt Schleier, was originally published in *Investor's Business Daily* on Sept. 20, 2002.

"Statesman Simon Bolívar: Dedication To Independence Made Him 'El Libertador,'" by J. Barnes, was originally published in *Investor's Business Daily* on June 27, 2001.

"President Andrew Jackson: Dedication To The Common Man Took Him To The Top," by Daniel Lindley, was originally published in *Investor's Business Daily* on Dec. 22, 1999.

"Statesman Winston Churchill: He Put His All Into The Effort To Win World War II," by J. Barnes, was originally published in *Investor's Business Daily* on May 31, 2000.

"Naval Giant Horatio Nelson: He Inspired His Men And Great Britain To Glory," by Matthew Robinson, was originally published in *Investor's Business Daily* on Jan. 12, 1998.

"Emperor Napoleon Bonaparte: How He Conquered Europe . . . And Surrendered It To Ego," by Peronet Despeignes, was originally published in *Investor's Business Daily* on Feb. 27, 1998.

"Sir Bernard Law Montgomery: This Commander Made Sure To Put His Men First," by Peter Benesh, was originally published in *Investor's Business Daily* on Aug. 14, 2003.

"President Ronald Reagan: This Persistent Populist Changed American Politics And Quashed Communism,"" by Cord Cooper, was originally published in *Investor's Business Daily* on May 21, 2002.

"Gen. Douglas MacArthur: His Focus Was Trained On Getting The Job Done," by Brian Mitchell, was originally published in *Investor's Business Daily* on March 12, 1999.

"Gen. Norman Schwarzkopf: Solid Dedication To Troops Makes Him An All-Time Great," by Jed Graham, was originally published in *Investor's Business Daily* on Feb. 25, 2004.

"Queen Elizabeth I: Reason And Moderation Marked Her Reign As One Of The Greatest," by Curt Schleier, was originally published in *Investor's Business Daily* on Oct. 6, 2000.

"Amnesty International's Ginetta Sagan: She Refused To Be Intimidated In Her Fight To Expose Human Rights Abuses," by George Neumayr, was originally published in *Investor's Business Daily* on May 3, 2001.

"Genghis Khan: Conqueror Won Wars, Minds," by Curt Schleier, was originally published in *Investor's Business Daily* on Feb. 11, 2004.

Index

About *Investor's Business Daily*

Investor's Business Daily provides critical, no-nonsense finance and investing information to nearly a million readers every day. Known for its innovative approach and straightforward analysis, it's one of today's most essential tools for empowering individual and institutional investors. Visit online at www.investors.com.